Masters of cinema

Francis Ford Coppola

CAHIERS DU CINEMA

Stéphane Delorme

Contents

Coppola on the set of *One from the Heart* (1982).

Introduction

The careers of all our iconic figures contain certain images that we prefer to suppress. One such is that of Francis Ford Coppola in 1971, then aged just thirty-two, on the set of *The Godfather*. In the middle of a chaotic shoot he has taken refuge in the toilet and is horrified to overhear some lowly technicians making fun of his incompetence and anticipating his replacement. He must have wondered why he had agreed to adapt a novel that didn't greatly excite him; like the directors of the French Nouvelle Vague who had revitalized the cinema of the old guard, he preferred to shoot original screenplays. No choice in Hollywood had seemed so improbable since Orson Welles directed *Citizen Kane* in 1941. And yet the young man overcame every difficulty, resolved every contradiction and put his name to the film that gave Hollywood a new lease of life, opening the door to all the angry young men — Scorsese, De Palma, Spielberg, Lucas and the rest — who are still making some of the best of America's films.

However, Coppola's greatness cannot be reduced to that one masterstroke. It runs its dazzling course through the box-office highs of the 1970s and lows of the 1980s, revealing an honesty and a regard for standards that are unparalleled. With each film Coppola questions his stylistic progress, in order to meet the demands of the subject in hand. The lyrical celebrant of 1960s rural teenage life, portrayed in *The Outsiders*, is as important as the wild megalomaniac directing *Apocalypse Now* through a megaphone in the jungle of the Philippines. This mixture of pride and humility is not the least paradoxical aspect of a body of work that, over this extreme disparity of styles, imposes a set of highly consistent obsessions: the individual, the family, power, relationship, youth and the drive to become a god — as evident in the seemingly antithetical *Dracula* and *Jack*, which share the same yearning for eternity.

Now that Coppola, after ten years in the wilderness, has recovered his 'nerve' with *Youth Without Youth* and *Tetro*, it is time to trace, step by step, the unpredictable career of a man who remains eternally young.

Sadie Frost and Anthony Hopkins in *Bram Stoker's Dracula* (1992).

Youth

From *Tonight for Sure* to *The Rain People*

To understand who I am, you'd have to understand the little five-year-old boy I was ... I was very passionate. I loved putting on plays for my friends, I loved to have them act together, and I think I'm still like that! ... That five-year-old Francis is certainly the best Francis there has ever been, and he's still there. In fact, I'm a survivor, I'm a child who has survived ...[1]

Francis Ford Coppola at the 1967
Cannes Film Festival.

First efforts

Francis Ford Coppola was born on 7 April 1939, in Detroit, Michigan, to Italia and Carmine Coppola. He had an older brother, August, whom he admired enormously, and a younger sister, Talia, who would later play the sister in *The Godfather* (1972), under the name Talia Shire. The job changes of Carmine Coppola, a flautist and conductor, meant that the family often moved house (Coppola still recalls his panicky fear of joining a class in the middle of a school year) before settling in the New York borough of Queens. When he was nine, an attack of polio meant he had to spend an entire year in bed. Half-paralysed and placed in quarantine, he entertained himself with an 8mm film projector, puppets and a television set. He turned himself into a ventriloquist and editor, happily putting together home movies, to which he added sound by using a tape recorder. When he came out of his seclusion, he showed his little gems to the neighbourhood children, charging them money to watch them. The film director and the businessman were born.

At first his heart was split between the theatre and film. In 1960 he graduated in theatre studies from Hofstra University, New York, where he had successfully written and directed plays. He headed west, and enrolled in what was then a very small film school at UCLA, in Los Angeles. Unlike his more pretentious fellow-students, he already had the intention of working in Hollywood. But at that time no film school had produced a director. How was he to bridge the gap?

He seized the first opportunity that offered itself: to make a 'nude' film, full of scantily clad actors, for the 'parallel' market. *The Peeper*, which is more comic than sexy, features a budding voyeur who spies on girls at the house of his neighbour, a photographer. A distributor showed an interest in it, on condition that the short feature was combined with an erotic Western that he had already, called *Wide Open Spaces*. Coppola complied, shot some additional scenes, asked his father to compose a jazzy score and brought out the full-length feature in 1961, under the title *Tonight for Sure*. Signed: Coppola. On the screen, young girls with names like Electra and Exotica frolic around topless while two boys reminisce over their misfortunes with the fair sex. It's not really erotic, but since nude films were doing brisk business, Coppola agreed on the same basis to shoot fifty minutes in colour, to be incorporated into a German black-and-white film. The result was *The Bellboy and the Playgirls*, which came out in 1962.

The independent producer Roger Corman[2] was looking for assistants at the time, and hired the eager young student as a jack-of-all-trades. After doing various lowly tasks, Coppola got the job of sound engineer on *The Young Racers* (1963), which Corman was shooting at the Liverpool Grand Prix. Since $20,000 was left over from the budget, his bold assistant suggested making a second film not far away, in Ireland, and that was the origin of *Dementia 13* (1963), shot in nine days, with a script written in three. Colleagues of Coppola's from UCLA joined him in a mad rush, among them Eleanor Neil, whom he married after the shoot. This gothic thriller is full of Hitchcockian themes: a mother haunted by the death of her daughter, drowned in a lake (*Rebecca*, 1940), a son who, in a flashback, realizes he was responsible for it (*Spellbound*, 1945), and a beautiful but greedy young woman who disappears after half an hour, cut to pieces with an axe (*Psycho*, 1960). The formula worked, and sex and violence were the order of the day. Corman was unhappy with the result, but had some scenes re-shot by a second unit in California. It was the end of their collaboration.

Left: William Campbell, Eithne Dunne and Bart Patton in *Dementia 13* (1963).

Below, left: Luana Anders in *Dementia 13* (1963).

Below: *Tonight For Sure* (1961).

Opposite page (both): *Battle Beyond the Sun* (1963).

The eye and the editing table

Roger Corman occupies a unique position in Hollywood. He was the first to understand the growing importance of teenage audiences and to produce one-hour-long films that teenagers watched at drive-ins. Sex and violence were part of the deal. His small business, AIP (the modest American International Pictures) thrived and launched young talents, giving them every kind of job. Coppola helped out first of all on a harebrained project, for which his experience as an uninhibited editor made him peculiarly suited: re-editing and dubbing a Soviet film bought from Mosfilm, Aleksandr Ptushko's *Sadko* (it had won the Silver Lion at Venice in 1953), under the improbable title *The Magic Voyage of Sinbad*. Nobody at AIP knew Russian, obviously, and the story was reinvented while watching the film. The boisterous drive-in audiences weren't surprised to see the Russian hero, now transformed into a blond Sinbad, spending his thousand and one nights dressed in furs.

Coppola took a bigger role in another aberration of AIP's, *Battle Beyond the Sun* (1963). It was originally a Soviet science-fiction film, describing the race to Mars by the two rival hemispheres, who have divided up the Earth between them. It was an overt allegory on the conquest of space, with a Communist flavour. Like a schoolboy prank, or some sort of Situationist hijacking, the propaganda film mutated into a monster movie. On Mars, a creature, entirely constructed by Coppola, attacks the Earthlings. The jump-cuts are horribly visible between the astronauts, dressed all in red, their mouths puckered in permanent smiles, and the monster, who does not hide his woes – a kind of eye stuck on a phallus, which soon joins battle with a giant 'vagina dentata'. It is hard to see how Coppola could have had such an idea, unless it was simply to amuse the teenagers, who were no fools.

The eye without a face will make a curious reappearance in several films (*The Godfather Part II*, 1974, and *Jack*, 1996), perhaps as a reference to the director's terrifying near-namesake Dr Coppelius in E.T.A. Hoffmann's story 'The Sandman', who steals little children's eyes. Sandman is also the name of one of the main characters in *The Cotton Club* (1984).

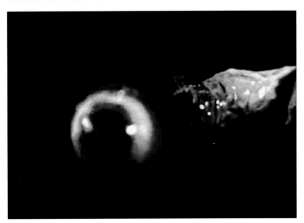

Off to Hollywood

Coppola was naturally disappointed, and jumped at the next opportunity that presented itself: a screenwriting contract with independent producers Seven Arts. Within a few months he had done every job there was. Seven Arts was an excellent school, so that unlike other directors of his generation, he started inside the system, which explains his rapid rise to fame and the confidence the studios had in him.[3] When Seven Arts joined up with Warner, Coppola sensed that his moment had arrived. He broke open his piggy-bank to make a start on *You're a Big Boy Now* (1966), and presented the studio with a fait accompli. Warner-Seven Arts were tempted, and came on board.

At the age of twenty-seven, then, he was directing for a studio a film he had written himself. '*You're a Big Boy Now* was regarded as nothing less than a miracle.'[4] His first 'serious' feature film is also Coppola's most light-hearted. France, freshness and fantasy: this zippy comedy is a tribute to the Nouvelle Vague. The hero traverses New York on roller-skates, has fun accosting passers-by as he goes, and smokes a cigarette while shaving, like Jean Paul Belmondo.

Poster for *You're a Big Boy Now* (1966) for the 1967 Cannes Film Festival.

Francis Ford Coppola in the 1960s.

Michael Dunn and Elizabeth Hartman in
You're a Big Boy Now (1966).

The brilliant opening sequence marks Coppola's real cinema debut: a dolly shot to the middle of a refectory reveals a great beanpole of a girl, against a background of rock music, who then forces the camera to move back out.

A speccy youth fantasizes over this Barbara Darling character — a student, model, actress and go-go dancer rolled into one. His demons pursue him through a rose-tinted New York, until he forms a slightly sadomasochistic relationship with the beauty. A conventionally dressed mummy's boy, he's the spitting image of Dustin Hoffman in *The Graduate* (1967), if we ignore the fact that Coppola's film was made first; and his suffocating parents represent a motif that will be quintessential, seen in a more favourable light — the family. *You're a Big Boy Now* was an entertaining stylistic exercise, but it was nevertheless chosen to represent the United States in competition at Cannes (it was the beginning of Coppola's adventures at the festival, with two 'palms' at stake), and from then on, Coppola had an air of the child prodigy about him.

The moment of hesitation on the part of the studios in the late 1960s was an ideal time for making a breakthrough. Against all expectations, this atypical disciple of two mentors, the Nouvelle

Francis Ford Coppola in the late 1960s.

Petula Clark and Fred Astaire in
12 *Finian's Rainbow* (1968).

Francis Ford Coppola with Petula Clark on
the set of *Finian's Rainbow* (1968).

Vague and Roger Corman, was offered the chance to make a musical with Fred Astaire and Petula Clark, *Finian's Rainbow* (1968). Coppola agreed, as much out of his genuine love for a 'book' he knew off by heart as to impress his father, who had introduced him to this Broadway classic. But he struggled to deal with a scatty but weak plot, and the studio's determination to turn it into a 'road show' (a long 70mm film with an interval) did this low-budget film no favours. Coppola's contribution lies mainly in the references to the Civil Rights movement, notably an unexpected sit-in, which bring the story up to date. The dazzling colour (in various shades of green) and the care taken over the songs meant that this modest film did not (completely) ruin Coppola's career, and he continued with his dogged, though always unsuccessful, attempts to make musicals, for example *One from the Heart* (1982) or the abandoned sung scripts of *The Cotton Club* (1984) and *Tucker* (1988). Coppola likes to tell people how, at twenty-eight, he was the youngest person on the set, but it was there that he met his future collaborator, George Lucas, who was even younger.[5]

Shirley Knight and James Caan
in *The Rain People* (1969).

Opposite page: Robert Duvall and Shirley Knight
in *The Rain People* (1969).

To San Francisco

The studio was happy with the way the job had been done. Coppola invested his fee in a more personal project and in buying equipment; throughout his career, the two would always go together. And here we go again! He led Warner — Seven Arts to believe that he was ready to begin shooting but that he needed more funds. The bluff worked, and he shot the film with the 'additional' funds.

The Rain People (1969) is based on what had happened to Coppola as a child, when his mother disappeared for a number of days. After making *Finian's Rainbow* to please his father, he seems to have made *The Rain People* 'for' his mother, as a way of solving the mystery of the days she spent far away from the family. A pregnant woman flees her marital home and on the road meets a former football player, who is dumb but endearing. Unable to cope with her pregnancy, she nevertheless finds herself taking care of an adult who behaves like a baby.

This road movie has the quality of a metaphor. The woman's unexplained flight at the beginning of the film prefigures the more radical wanderings of Barbara Loden's *Wanda* (1970),

and what follows in the vein of classic patterns is
more suggestive of Martin Scorsese's *Alice Doesn't
Live Here Anymore* (1973) — to compare it with the
two great road movies of the period whose prota-
gonists are women. The most inspired moments
all have to do with withdrawal, like the long tele-
phone conversation in which the sound editor,
Walter Murch, who had worked on *THX 1138*,
lays the sound of the actress's voice as it would
be heard through the handset over the shot of
her talking. The dissociation of sound and image,
and the idea of separation from oneself, would be
heightened in *The Conversation* (1974), another case
of self-seclusion on the part of a solitary man who
has withdrawn from the world.

Although it may have shown too strongly
the influence of modern European cinema, the
film was well received. More importantly, *The Rain
People* is the first example of the challenge that
every shoot would now represent for Coppola.
Thanks to the success of Dennis Hopper's *Easy Rider*
(1969), he was able to persuade Warner to allow the
film to be shot on location: eight vehicles left New
York for a period of eight weeks, travelling as far as
Nebraska, where the crew stayed for two months.
The 'caravan' included a studio and an editing suite
(the rushes were developed in Hollywood and sent
back within three days), confirming Coppola's high
degree of autonomy. The experience of editing in
Ogallala, Nebraska, convinced him that he needed
to distance himself from Hollywood if he wanted
to go on working with minimal interference.

While visiting San Francisco, he found
the perfect spot, just the right distance from Los
Angeles. It was there, in the spring of 1969, that he
moved in with his buddies George Lucas and Walter
Murch to set up American Zoetrope. Then he could
begin to think on a grand scale. His mind full of
the idea of conquest, he saw Zoetrope as not only
a place of resistance, but also one in competition
with Hollywood: a haven that would bring together

keen young graduates from UCLA, a paradise for budding directors. Since he could not do without the support of a studio, he bluffed Warner again, offering to help them finance his company's first seven films, starting with George Lucas's *THX 1138*.[6] The youngster's cheek earned him the contract. But this euphoria did not last long; the studio hated Lucas's feature film so much that they demanded full repayment of their investment. In November 1970, Warner withdrew support, and Zoetrope was in debt for years. The first phase of Coppola's career had come to an end.

He was still in the process of 'rising from the ashes', and was saved by a screenplay he had co-written in 1966 that was only now being turned into a film: *Patton*. In 1971, he won the Oscar for best screenplay, which was enough to renew the confidence of the studios.

At the Height of His Powers

From *The Godfather* to *Apocalypse Now*

Marlon Brando in *The Godfather* (1972).

Following pages: Salvatore Corsitto and Marlon Brando in *The Godfather* (1972).

A casting error

No matter how talented Coppola was as a screen-writer, how ambitious as a director or how bold as an individual, the question remains: how were the studios able to offer *The Godfather* to an almost unknown filmmaker? Paramount origi-nally planned to make a not-too-expensive film (with a budget of $2.5 million), based on a suc-cessful novel. It seemed sensible to choose a docile director, who would be able to make it quickly; an Italian-American would give the project an addi-tional guarantee. Coppola's name suggested itself. Very soon, the novel's growing success doubled the pressure, while the director's wish (in which he was indulged) to recreate the 1940s, instead of bringing the novel up to date, doubled the budget.

And how, again, are we to explain the fact that this young director suddenly developed such breadth and ambition? *The Godfather* brings off the feat of being at the same time in the tradition of great classic sagas (like, for example, Luchino Visconti's *The Leopard*, 1963), and totally in tune with the spirit of its time. We have lost sight now of its revolutionary innovations, and we need to remember them. The shadowy cinematography of cameraman Gordon Willis plunges us into a secret

world. We may praise its restraint, but at the time that restraint shouted in your face. The studio bosses complained that they couldn't see anything during these long conversations filmed in semi-darkness. Walter Murch's mixing of the music makes the crime scenes completely silent, and uses a mournful lament in the shots that follow them. The violence explodes in cold, spectacular bursts that burn themselves into one's memory: the horse's head slipped into the blood-stained bed of a recalcitrant studio boss, or the murder of Sonny, riddled with bullets next to his car, an echo of Arthur Penn's *Bonnie and Clyde* (1967) or Andy Warhol's screen prints of automobile accidents.

Shadows, silence, violence: the director's inventions are at the service of a canvas that aspires to be measured on a mythical scale. It traces, in two hours and fifty-five minutes, the fall and rise of two godfathers, a father and a son, Vito (Brando) and his youngest son Michael (Pacino), two characters always 'on the point of' (growing up, dying): we have here the matrix of all of Coppola's work. They are accompanied by three 'sons': the eldest, the headstrong Sonny (Caan); the second, Fredo (Cazale), a slightly cowardly playboy; and the German-Irish *consigliere*, the Godfather's spiritual son (Duvall), who is admirably cool despite not having the blood of the Don in his veins. Snubbed at first, Michael asserts himself in a terrific scene in which he takes his wounded father to hospital. At the beginning, he could express his disgust for the crimes of the Mafia and say to Kay (Diane Keaton), his future wife: 'That's my family, it's not me.' From that moment, he has become the family.

James Caan, Marlon Brando, Al Pacino and John Cazale in *The Godfather* (1972).

A genealogy of evil

The Godfather is a story of damnation. All we need do is compare the parallel editing of the two celebrations and simultaneous crimes, at the beginning and ending of the film. The opening, which has become a classic, shows us, on the one hand, the family in the garden, celebrating the marriage of Connie, the godfather's daughter, and, on the other, her father doing business in his dark office. The editing reveals the 'boss' hidden under the domestic surface and a murky world, behind the scenes, both peacefully co-existing.

By the end of the film, things are very different. As Connie's son is being baptized, Michael's henchmen eliminate the heads of the five rival families. Here again, a ceremony serves to mask atrocities, except that this time the crime is not simply the converse of the celebration, but its contradiction. There is an absolute contradiction between the priest's question to Michael, the baby's godfather, 'Do you renounce Satan?', and the extraordinarily violent acts Michael has ordered to be carried out. He lies; he has lost his soul. The massacre will engulf his own brother-in-law; the family is no longer safe. The Don has turned into a despot.

Michael is a tragic figure. With a boss's natural authority, he gets his way, like a free man. And yet it all weighs on him. With a pensive expression, his shoulders bent under heavy responsibilities, he carries the burden of a fate that is too much for him. His transformation into a war machine is accompanied by the sad waltz tune composed by Nino Rota; he gropes his way forwards in his father's shadow, because he seems 'to have been

Al Pacino and Marlon Brando in
The Godfather (1972).

Improvising a masterpiece

The glorious set of people who made *The Godfather* started out looking like a reserve team: after a series of flops, Brando was *persona non grata*; Al Pacino (whom the producer, Robert Evans, described as a 'little troll') had nothing but Jerry Schatzberg's *The Panic in Needle Park* (1971) to his name (the studio wanted Robert Redford!); James Caan and Robert Duvall had made their debuts in *The Rain People*; and Gordon Willis, later Woody Allen's cinematographer, had an almost blank CV, with only Alan J. Pakula's *Klute* (1971) to boast about. For the rest, Coppola turned to his family (his sister plays Connie, Michael Corleone's sister) and he has described *The Godfather* as 'a film about a family, made by a family'. The appropriation of the project by this young man freshly dropped into the system seems almost incredible. But very soon,

the wind changed, and the shoot turned into a battle of wills. At risk of being fired at any moment, Coppola had to demonstrate a variety of skills, including improvisation and belt-tightening.

First of all, Gordon Willis was promoted and set himself up as a rival to the director, advocating the classical virtues of straightforward, no-frills filming as against the stylized approach that Coppola was looking for. The cinematography of *The Godfather* is the product of that two-headed monster. But before long, pressure from the studios (who went so far as to appoint a 'substitute' director to keep a surreptitious eye on things) ensured that they all pulled together. Financial constraints meant that the film had to be shot quickly, using two cameras. The dramatic death of the Godfather, playing in the garden with his grandson before he collapses into

a bed of tomatoes, was improvised with two cameras during a lunch break, and is quite unlike the rest of the film. The remarkably 'dense' scene of his funeral brings the Corleone family face to face with those who have betrayed it in a straightforward series of high- and low-angle shots and reverse shots. You could cut the tension with a knife, but on the day of filming, Coppola wept with rage, sitting on a gravestone, because he could not shoot the scene the way he wanted to.

But improvisation went even further than that, because some scenes were missing. The powerful reunion of Kay and Michael was filmed several weeks later, with another cinematographer, and is a complete mismatch with the rest of the film. The same goes for the final conversation between Michael and his father, which was added because there was no scene

with just the two actors in it, and Robert Towne, the screenwriter of Roman Polanski's *Chinatown* (1974), was given the job of writing it. Most of these modified, improvised or additional scenes come one after another in the second half of *The Godfather*. This extraordinary degree of fragmentation has a tremendous effect, not unlike that of Kubrick's cinema, as if each scene was a classic in itself. A self-styled masterpiece of impassivity, *The Godfather* is like a necklace made up of stones of different sizes and colours, and is reminiscent of the cobbled-together methods of the Corman school.

Francis Ford Coppola with Marlon Brando and Al Pacino on the set of *The Godfather* (1972).

Al Pacino in *The Godfather Part II* (1974).

made for that' from time immemorial. From one Corleone to the next, through their various vendettas, we accompany the family from within, like a little Sicilian island, floating tragically above the law and above morality.[7] Even more surprisingly on the part of a director of the 1960s generation, there is no reference to the economic and political aspects of the Mafia, a word that is never uttered. Capitalism is a modern system for gaining power, a playground; it is not capitalism that is the Evil.[8]

This achievement says much about Coppola's work. It is a romantic panorama of one man's powers, desires and excesses, including the ultimate risk of losing love and family, a great resurrection of ancient myths rather than a critical treatment of the history of his times. To break the law is one thing, to harm one's nearest and dearest is another. The sequel confirms this emphasis on the family: the worst sin of the entire trilogy is the murder of

a brother, like Cain's murder of Abel, not the series of crimes carried out one after the other.

By the end of the shoot, Coppola was weary, and launched himself into another exhausting commission, an adaptation of *The Great Gatsby*,[9] which prevented him, ironically, from enjoying the unexpected success of a film he had thought was doomed to fail. The young prodigy won the Oscar for best film for *The Godfather*. Soon afterwards, he produced *American Graffiti* (1973), directed by George Lucas, and this resounding new success made him a multimillionaire. This was the first time that young directors had seized power in Hollywood, and the first time they had earned so much money. Within the space of a few weeks, the films of Coppola, Lucas and William Friedkin (*French Connection*, 1971; *The Exorcist*, 1973), and soon Steven Spielberg too (*Jaws*, 1975), became the most successful of all time. *The Godfather* occupies 25 a decidedly unusual place on that list: it was the only one not to succumb to the siren song of 'entertainment'.

A bitter figure

For the sequel to *The Godfather*, Coppola was given free rein and twice the budget ($11 million), which enabled him to travel to Nevada, Los Angeles and Cuba, since the Cuban revolution was the setting for this second part.

The Godfather Part II (1974) takes a very bold approach: to show in parallel the life of Michael, the new godfather, and that of his father, Vito Corleone,[10] in the 1910s and 1920s. Although the film begins with Vito's childhood, that strand is nested inside the other one, so that Michael's rise and fall form the principal theme, which the second joins like a solo on the flute. As the film proceeds, Vito's ordinary beginnings provide a heroic parallel to Michael's slow descent into Hell. Youth and maturity, hope and disillusion, seem like the two sides of a medal, its face and reverse showing the same individual at two different ages.

But there is a profound difference: Vito thinks in terms of an exchange of services, based on an archaic paradigm in which the boss embodies the law for the common good; Michael shuts himself up in his ivory tower, turning away friends and enemies in his increasing paranoia. The remarkable epilogue, in which a flashback shows Michael enlisting in the army against everybody's advice, and sitting at a table by himself, summarizes his life up to this point: he's a temperamental child who puts his own interests above those of the

Robert De Niro and Leopoldo Trieste in *The Godfather Part II* (1974).

family. His development was predictable from the first episode: the way in which he distances himself from the others at the wedding ('That's my family, Kay, it's not me') and then changes tack as if he is the 'favourite son', excluding the *consigliere* and then Kay, in whose face he ruthlessly shuts a door. The entire trajectory sketched in the first part is magisterially rounded out in the second.

The young Sicilian we see arriving at Ellis Island in 1901 is the epitome of the immigrants who 'believe in America'; Michael's America is no more than a factitious paradise, lacking any historical or geographical identity. Against all probability, he leaves his New York fiefdom for Nevada, a simulacrum of the West of the pioneers, where he holes up on his ranch, with its extreme security measures.

And here he is at Lake Tahoe, surrounded by a shady bunch of people who have no connection with the 100 per cent Italian-American family in the wedding scene of the first episode. This intrusion by WASP (white Anglo-Saxon Protestant) America is first represented visually by the blondness of the guests — young, privileged people who will be America's future.[11] The party swarms with politicians of doubtful probity, adversaries who are more serious (in a different way) than the strutting local mobsters supplanted by Vito as his life evolves in parallel. A senator insults the 'greasy-haired Wops' in Michael's office. There is a violent contrast between the sanctuary of *The Godfather*, where Don Corleone received visitors as if in a confessional, and this office with its open window and its view of the hangers-on, disporting themselves

Al Pacino (right) in *The Godfather Part II* (1974).

in the sun. The sense of the sacred has been lost; everything that made the Mafia a religion, and the Godfather a holy man whose hand one kissed, has evaporated in the oblique western light. The property itself has become a fortified compound, surrounded absurdly by electric fences, which pose no challenge to the intruders who come and machine-gun Michael in his own bed.

The Cuban revolution provides the background for the Judas kiss that Michael bestows on Fredo, the brother who has betrayed him: 'You broke my heart', he keeps saying. The family tragedy eclipses the historical setting, all the more so since here Coppola alludes to his own life — his relationship with his brother, and his marriage. The myth is never more powerful than when it draws on the director's own experience. Michael is always a self-portrait, developed to the point of exaggeration in *The Godfather Part III* (1990), for which Coppola retained hardly any of his actors except Pacino, his sister Talia and his daughter Sofia.

The Godfather Part II ends with a close-up of a pensive Michael, a prisoner of his inner emptiness. It's a shot that cannot be precisely dated (his hair is slightly grey) and could be read as showing him years later, as though he had spent all these years motionless, waiting for death. It explains why Coppola long refused to make a third Godfather film. How was he to follow that shot? Michael is a lonely, melancholy figure, full of bitterness, defeated and turned in on himself. The Don sitting in his chair, the emblem of power, has become the very image of impotence. All the last part of the film has led up to this image: the sudden snowfall on his return from Cuba, and Michael, isolated in his internal exile, filmed through the windows of the house, which is gradually being overgrown by flowers and ferns. Vito's youth retrospectively takes on all its force, giving a temporal depth to the imaginary space of Lake Tahoe. Something — running counter to his mad flight to Nevada — makes Michael want to make up for lost time. It's a movement that chimes with the words that Vito whispers to his little boy: 'Michael, your father loves you very much', words of which we are reminded just before the final shot, as we recall the powerful image of Vito making his son wave goodbye from the train, as if he were a puppet.[12] He's saying goodbye to us, he's leaving the film. Michael has become the Evil, but he is no more than a puppet, manipulated by ancestral violence.

Listening

The melancholy transition from *The Godfather* to The *Godfather Part II* cannot be understood if a piece is removed from the board: *The Conversation*, made between the two, in 1974. Following *The Godfather*, which he saw as a commercial contract, Coppola was eager to make a film of which he would be the creator in his own right. In 1966 he had started work on *The Conversation*, fascinated by technical developments in the field of espionage, in particular the art of carrying out surveillance in a crowd, using long-range microphones. We recognize here the first sequence, in which Harry Caul monitors the conversation of a couple who are carrying on an illicit affair, as they walk through Union Square in San Francisco.

The film appears to be the diametrical opposite of *The Godfather*. It is the story of a man who is brilliant at his job but emotionally inadequate, who finds himself embroiled in a case that is beyond his grasp and that drives him deeper into his state of torpor. Gene Hackman, with his closed-down features, moustache and grey raincoat, answers with resignation to the name Caul. This professional has no sort of grandeur about him as he carries out his commissions as if with his eyes shut, too wary to confide in anyone, whether it be his competitors, friends or mistresses. But there's a crack in his armour: his professional activities once caused the deaths of a woman and a child, and when another case threatens to take a similar turn, he falls prey to his inner demons. What is this case? He is hired by a big businessman and, while listening to a couple's conversation, hears the man let fall this ambiguous sentence: 'He'd kill us if he had the chance.' Instead of delivering the tapes, Caul listens to them in search of a clue, but is unable to

Gene Hackman in *The Conversation* (1974).

prevent the murder taking place. His failure is all the more catastrophic since he gets the murder wrong: the couple are the authors of the plot, not the victims.

An error, a guilty conscience, neurotic repetition: the scenario seems closer to Brian De Palma than to Coppola's flights of grandeur. And *The Conversation* happens to be one of De Palma's favourite films; he quotes it explicitly in *Blow Out* (1981), in which a recording engineer witnesses the murder of a politician. The two films have a common source: Michelangelo Antonioni's *Blow-Up* (1966), in which a photographer captures the image of a murder without realizing it. All three films share the same motifs: a lonely man shuts himself up in his workroom in order to retrieve what he had failed to see; his frantic efforts produce evidence but are not enough to save the people under threat; the would-be detective, buried in the detail, withdraws from the world into a parallel reality. He knows everything, but is unable to bring this knowledge into the real world. These men, like the photographer in the final shot of *Blow-Up*, disappear.[13]

The Conversation moves from disconnection (Caul does his spying from his van, invisibly) to paralysis (he had been paralysed as a child, just like Coppola when he had polio). When he locates the crime, Caul finally has a chance to act, but faced with murder he is so helpless he prefers to shut himself up in his room. Even the facts lack a firm basis in reality. The crime is shown in such a fantastical way that we doubt it ever took place: a woman strangled with a shower-curtain, a flushed toilet that brings up litres of blood: we're suddenly in the world of *Psycho* and horror films. We never know how the crime was committed, and only a sick imagination provides us with an improbable version.

The Conversation has often been put in the context of the decline in American political life, from the assassination of John F. Kennedy in 1963 to the Watergate scandal in 1972. Of Dallas, Coppola recalls less the assassination itself than the film broadcast on television over and over again, just as Harry Caul repeatedly plays the tapes on his machine. Of Watergate, Coppola remembers the visual surveillance less than the presidential tapes. He has ultimately retained no memory of the political implications of these two events, but only the technical details, as though for him the real revolution of those years was an aesthetic one: on the one hand, the idea of rewinding and obsessive repetition, and on the other, of listening and interpreting. *The Conversation* has nothing in common with paranoid conspiracy films such as Alan J. Pakula's *All the President's Men* (1975), further evidence that for Coppola the personal is more important than the political.

Right after he had finished filming, Coppola began *The Godfather Part II* and gave Walter Murch carte blanche as far as editing and dubbing were concerned; Murch made the whole film into a conversational 'loop'.[14] But the most important thing had perhaps happened earlier. The couple stop at a bench on which a homeless man is lying. 'Oh look, that's terrible. Oh God! Every time I see one of those old guys, I always think the same thing. I always think that he was once somebody's baby boy … And he had a mother and a father who loved him. And now, there he is, half-dead on a park bench and where is his mother or his father or his uncles now?' Caul listens to these words again in his deep loneliness, and we have the feeling that they're talking about him. This old man on the bench, who hears the conversation without understanding it, is identified with the spy in the raincoat, one more person riding on this crowded carousel. Harry Caul is as disconnected as this homeless man because he is a man without a family. And the 'ultimate' man without a family (which a homeless man on a bench is, in his own way) is Michael Corleone at the end of *The Godfather Part II*. But he, too, was once somebody's baby boy.

The Conversation — a black hole between the two *Godfathers*, a story in a 'grey area', about an impotent expert — reveals by juxtaposition the vanity of the hungry, driven Corleone family. It demonstrates that melancholy is the underlying emotion in these films, which so often appear to be affectless. Look at Harry Caul: sitting on his sofa, he starts playing the umpteenth jazz number on his saxophone, alone, permanently alone, just like Michael, sitting in his chair at the end of *The Godfather Part II*. In four films, the Coppola of the 1970s has portrayed four men who are consumed by melancholy.

Better than Disneyland

The fourth film, obviously, was *Apocalypse Now* (1979), Coppola's 'magic mountain', which we must have the courage to climb with him — a colossal film that nobody could have expected from the newly acknowledged prodigy. But that's how Coppola proceeds, without preconceptions, choosing for his next project something as different as possible from the previous one. His last three films were dark, sober, serious? Then let's dive into the jungle for a big firework show. As we hear him say in *Hearts of Darkness: A Filmmaker's Apocalypse*, the documentary that his wife, Eleanor, made during the shoot: 'This movie I'm making is not in the tradition of the great Max Ophuls or David Lean vein. This movie was made in the tradition of Irwin Allen.' (Irwin Allen is a director of spectacular disaster movies.) It's in that context that *Apocalypse Now* should be judged: as a disaster movie, an apocalypse movie, delivering scenes of catastrophic action one after another, with no coherent plot.

It was a big, popular film, as was *The Godfather* in the genre of melodrama, but this time made with the world's teenagers in mind, a sort of high-class Corman to be shown outdoors, with plenty of sex and violence. Coppola even had the wild idea of building a cinema bang in the centre of the United States, just to screen *Apocalypse Now*. The film would be shown nowhere else, and people would come to 'visit' it from all over the world, the way they come to visit Mount Rushmore. That shows how much he wanted to build a monument — and the extent of his megalomania.

All that apart, *Apocalypse Now* is a film about the Vietnam War. The screenplay written by George Lucas and John Milius in the late 1960s had been lying in a drawer at Zoetrope, and Lucas, who had started making *Star Wars*, let it languish a little longer. Coppola picked it up again with Milius and decided to turn it into an adaptation of Joseph Conrad's *Heart of Darkness*. A departure from the historical truth about Vietnam, it is the first sign

Francis Ford Coppola at home in Napa Valley in the late 1970s.

Opposite page: *Apocalypse Now* (1979).

of the 'romanticizing' impulse that always carries Coppola far beyond the bounds of reality. How, after all, are we to reconcile the moral enigma of *Heart of Darkness* with this apocalyptic entertainment? That is the major disjuncture of *Apocalypse Now*, what makes it fascinating, even though its elements cannot be reconciled. Captain Willard's journey up-river, on a mission to execute Colonel Kurtz, who has installed himself in Cambodia as an unbridled despot, consists of two very distinct strands: on the one hand, we hear Willard's inner thoughts, delivered in voice-over as he reads the dossier on Kurtz, as he travels upstream before coming face to face with him in a grandiloquent finale that combines literature and philosophy, and on the other, the alarming sights that accompany each stop on the river, from Colonel Kilgore (Robert Duvall) bombing a village to make a place where he can surf, to the scantily clad Playboy Bunnies dancing for the overexcited soldiers. Each stop has its particular theme-park attraction. 'Fuck, man, this is better than Disneyland', says one of the soldiers, his face painted with khaki, in a cloud of pink artificial smoke.

How are we to link introspection and spectacle? This metaphysical show stands up until the finale, when the introspection itself becomes spectacular: the literal 'head-banging' of Kurtz (Marlon Brando) is legendary, so determined was Coppola to film only that, the shaven scalp moving in and out of the darkness, and Brando's hand stroking it. Many critics have said 'the apocalypse is a let-down',[15] and the finale doesn't match the build-up of expectation, even though from the opening images it's a dazzling portrayal of inner turmoil, and Coppola has the courage to set a limit on the spectacle, reducing it to a bar-room brawl. But what a brawl! Kurtz quotes T. S. Eliot's 'The Hollow Men' and calls everything — himself, Willard, Vietnam — vanity, emptiness. It cannot be disputed that at this point Coppola is developing further the portrait of Michael Corleone, whom he left meditating in his chair. Is Kurtz insane? It doesn't matter; he's a melancholic. He is withdrawn, lying on his straw mattress; to enter his cave is like penetrating Christ's tomb. Not enough note has been taken of the fact that he also gives Willard a mission: to kill him, yes, but more importantly, to let his son know what has become of his father. That is why Willard, a messenger again, has to leave Kurtz's hideout in the final shots. There's no doubt that Coppola has blind faith in that act of handing down — the father, exhausted and having lost everything, still has something to tell his son: that loss itself. When he is left with nothing else, he still has something to hand down to him.[16]

An adventure film

All this is a very long way from Vietnam. That's the main charge made by Stanley Kubrick, who sees Kurtz as a kind of King Kong (and he's not far wrong), and Brian De Palma, who sees him as Attila the Hun[17] (he's not wrong, either). One could equally well mention the Minotaur. Offer Coppola something real, and he'll bring out the mythical in it, so it's difficult to make that the charge against him. After all, does *Apocalypse Now* tell us any less about Vietnam than Michael Cimino's melodramatic *The Deer Hunter* (1978),

which had been released earlier (but did not enjoy its great success until later) than Oliver Stone's *Platoon* (1987), which sees things entirely in black and white, or the rather abstract *Full Metal Jacket*, shot in London by Kubrick in 1987? *Apocalypse Now* is an acid trip, seen through a floating, druggy lens, but it takes on board one of the realities of war — its confusion. 'Do you know who's in command here?', repeats the exhausted Willard, until a soldier replies, 'Yeah', with no further comment. Nobody is in command, the army has been decapitated, America has lost its grasp.

Walter Murch's tricks of the trade

Yet in *Apocalypse Now*, you're right, actors look into the camera quite often and it seems to integrate effortlessly into the flow of the film. The curious thing is that I've never read or heard anyone talk about it – it's never referred to in any studies about the film, even though it breaks one of the cardinal rules of filmmaking. In that briefing scene where Willard gets his mission, the characters are looking straight at the camera when they talk to Willard. If they are doing that, the mathematically correct thing would be to have Willard looking at the camera too. Instead he's looking to the left side of the lens, which is correct according to conventional film grammar. Yet you never feel the general is looking at the audience: you believe he's looking at Willard. But when Willard finally does look at the camera, at the end of the scene, you feel he's looking at us – at the audience – and thinking: *Can you believe this?*

I guess it has to do with the intense subjectivity of the film: the fact that Willard is the eyes and ears through which we comprehend this war, and through whose sensibilities the war is going to be filtered.

But there was a problem waiting for me: the departure from the French plantation had been shot only once and showed the dock in its pre-ruined state. There was no departure with a ruined dock. You couldn't arrive in ruins and depart with the dock all fixed up! So if we used the ruined-dock material to get into the sequence, I couldn't get out. Then, in combing through the raw material, I found a shot with Martin Sheen – Willard – and Aurore Clément where she gets out of bed, undresses, and closes the mosquito netting all around the bed. There was something beautifully evocative about seeing her silhouetted against the mosquito netting, and I thought, She looks

like a ghost, and the mosquito netting looks like fog.
It was *then* that I made the connection. If we began the French plantation later, if we let Chief's grief for Clean's death take us into the fog that overwhelms the boat, when the fog begins to lift, there are the ruins of the plantation, as if Willard and the crew had gone back in time. Then the film could get into what Francis described as the Buñuel-like ghostliness of the dinner discussion, people stuck forever in the political passions of the early 1950s, which were a mirror image of the American involvement in Vietnam fifteen years later.
What originally happened next is that Willard grabbed her and pulled her through the mosquito netting, they made love, and – as in the script – you found them the next morning. But in this version the image of Aurore dissolves away and you're left with the disembodied silhouette

of this woman, hovering against a milky-white background. Then you realize you're back on the boat, where you started.
When I discovered that transition, which was not intended in the script, something unlocked for me. I felt that I was beginning to grasp the language of this new version.

This is an extract from *The Conversations: Walter Murch and the Art of Editing Film*, by Michael Ontdaatje Knopf, New York, 2002.

Harrison Ford and Martin Sheen in *Apocalypse Now* (1979).

Top: *Apocalypse Now* (1979).

Bottom: Robert Duvall in *Apocalypse Now* (1979).

Martin Sheen (below) and Sam Bottoms (right) in
Apocalypse Now (1979).

Francis Ford Coppola with Marlon Brando on the set of
Apocalypse Now (1979).

Every colonel (like Kilgore) behaves like a despot, and Kurtz is no more than a monstrous caricature of them, the living statue of a deity. The staff officers are in Saigon, eating good food, living like civilians, far from the realities of the jungle. That is the meaning of the long scene in which Willard receives his orders. As Kurtz's recorded voice says, 'There is nothing I detest more than the stench of lies', the beef being served up to these skivers is shown in close-up, and when we learn that Willard kills Kurtz with a machete, in a sequence edited in parallel with one showing the slaughter of a cow, this meat takes on a special savour.

The sardonic humour here needs to be emphasized; it is not a frequent feature of Coppola's work. Kilgore, standing there in his cavalry hat, coming out with 'I love the smell of napalm in the morning' and the absurd statement 'Charlie [the Viet Cong] don't surf': everyone can quote these lines balanced between humour and horror. The seriousness of Kurtz's 'the horror, the

horror' is counterbalanced by the comedy of the court jester (Dennis Hopper), an acid-tripping photographer. As in all his films, Coppola adapts his style to his subject, but this habit now takes him to the edge. If the subject is confusion, how is he to maintain a modicum of order? Coppola goes far, because more or less consciously he puts himself in a situation of disorder, even danger. Life and film have to coincide, and Coppola was able to say, at the Cannes Festival, 'My movie is not about Vietnam, my movie is Vietnam.' He went off to film in the Philippines, and had to handle Filipino army helicopters, build a village (and rebuild it completely after a typhoon), substitute Martin Sheen for Harvey Keitel, suspend the shoot after Martin Sheen's heart attack, and so on. He was not responsible for these events, of course, but the absurd way in which the shoot got held up and lasted over a year, and the film took three years to make, was partly due to his thirst for adventure. He admits that he saw himself as Kurtz, and took

Francis Ford Coppola with Robert Duvall on the set of
Apocalypse Now (1979).

advantage of his power, bogged down as he was in the back of beyond. It is remarkable that the ending, which attracted so much criticism, is actually so slow, with a soldier in the background doing tai-chi, as if one had reached the lowest point of entropy. The disorder is such that we keep on falling, right into Kurtz's dark lair, the only point in the film at which time stops.

The two years that it took to edit *Apocalypse Now* represent a Titanic effort. Several teams worked on the rushes, and on the music. The confusion that had reigned in the jungle now invaded the studios. The most successful piece of editing is, without doubt, the attack on the village, to the sound of Wagner's 'Ride of the Valkyries'; in the midst of chaos, the action remains crystal clear. Coppola has never been happy with the 1979 version, which lasted 2 hours and 33 minutes; in 2001, with Walter Murch's help, he made a version for cinema release that ran for 3 hours and 12 minutes: *Apocalypse Now Redux*.[18]

Only ten years separate the making of *You're a Big Boy Now* and *Apocalypse Now*, showing what tremendous progress Coppola had made. His work took on a new scope and stature, and his professional success was dizzying. He had to his credit one of the most successful films ever, *The Godfather*, which took $134 million in box-office receipts in the United States alone; he had won two Palmes d'Or (for *The Conversation* and *Apocalypse Now*) and a handful of Oscars; and the predicted disaster of *Apocalypse Now* had turned into the goose that laid the golden eggs, taking $78 million in the United States. Without this heroic picture of a man crowned with every success, it is impossible to understand the adventures — to call them rash would be an understatement — on which he was about to embark. The first was Zoetrope, an old project (perhaps his life's project), which took on new life; the second, *One from the Heart* (1982), a crazy idea — to make an electronic musical.

Maturity

From *One from the Heart* to *Tucker*

Nastassja Kinski in *One from the Heart* (1982).

Right: Hans-Jürgen Syberberg, Francis Ford Coppola, Werner Herzog and Dusan Makavejev at the Coppola Napa Valley home in the 1980s.

The Utopia of Zoetrope

After *Apocalypse Now*, it was time to go home. Coppola didn't exactly take a warrior's well-earned rest, that's not his style. 'Home' was the Sentinel Building, the headquarters of Zoetrope, which the despot of the jungle now took in hand again, using strong-arm tactics on his return from the battleground. The communal, hippie dream was over, and Zoetrope became its founder's creature.

Another dream was put in its place: a utopian community of great film directors. Coppola opened his home to European *auteurs*: Werner Herzog, Wim Wenders and Hans-Jürgen Syberberg spent vacations at his property in Napa Valley. He took on distributing Syberberg's *Hitler* (1977) and Abel Gance's *Napoléon* (1927) in the United States, and in 1978 he began the long and difficult production of Wim Wenders's *Hammett* (1982).[19]

One important piece was missing from the board: in 1980, Coppola provided his company with studios, buying the venerable Hollywood General Studios. Zoetrope grew out of all proportion. He now had a base in Hollywood itself, and wanted to compete in the life of the 'dream factory' on his own turf. It is difficult to imagine that a man who had literally 'gone beyond' cinema (by

way of myth, literature or opera) should confine himself to it in the way of pure cinephiles such as Spielberg, Scorsese or Lucas. It is difficult to imagine the adventurous Coppola following in the footsteps of his more introvert friend George Lucas, founder of the Lucasfilm studios. But his obsession with control was such that he wanted to have everything within his grasp. That megalomania drove him to revise completely the processes by which films were made. He put his close associates on the payroll, as if they were in a theatre company. He became as much a businessman as a film director, and the first work produced by the 'factory' (*One from the Heart*), looked very much like a prototype designed to showcase the technical innovations of which he had made himself a master.

A laboratory

One from the Heart retains Coppola's inordinate ambition, but applies it to a tiny story, at the other end of the scale from epic. It's a reversal that typifies the spirit of the 1980s, years of a retreat from the epic to the personal, but also, in parallel with that, a period of expansion of the image towards a mythology of the image. Here it takes the form of a love story between two anonymous people in Las

43

Vegas (played by Teri Garr and Frederic Forrest), who separate and get back together. A regular commentary on their feelings is provided by a duo heard only on the soundtrack: Tom Waits and the country singer Crystal Gayle.

We have retained the utopian idea of 'electronic cinema' and have included many fantasies under the term. But if we listen to what Coppola says, and if we look closely at the film, we'll see that something else entirely is at stake. What he wanted was to make a live TV show, an unedited film that would, as it were, effortlessly unroll its 'seamless garment', to use André Bazin's expression. The confusion arose from the fact that the reality filmed has nothing about it of either an official or a natural version of reality — the city of Las Vegas with its neon signs — and that the editing and lighting effects are ostentatious. But when one looks at the film again, what stands out are the sequence-length shots that follow the characters, and the theatrical devices that let us move from one space to another in the same shot.

Teri Garr in *One from the Heart* (1982).

Through a transparent wall we catch sight of what is happening in the next room, false partitions allow us to pass through spaces. The use of the Steadicam[20] gives us wings. At the very moment when he was extolling the virtues of electronic transformation, what Coppola really wanted was to make theatre.

The grand circus of *One from the Heart* appealed to few people. The fierce New York critic Pauline Kael wrote, 'This movie isn't from the heart, but from the lab.' In other words, it's not a love story, but an ad. It is true that the characters are like balls in a pinball machine, and the closest visual comparison is perhaps *Tron* (1982), produced by Walt Disney. But, after all, wasn't that already the case of the soldiers in *Apocalypse Now*? Dropped into a war that goes on without them, in their little motor boat, they are crazily moving bodies, crashing from one bank to the other, like the balls in the arcade game. *One from the Heart* reveals a truth about Coppola's films: they contain nothing that could be called an 'outdoors'.

Raul Julia in *One from the Heart* (1982).

Francis Ford Coppola on the set of
One from the Heart (1982).

The hangar in *The Conversation*, the ranch in *The Godfather Part II*, the jungle and Las Vegas are places of seclusion. Coppola has too readily been seen as a maker of films about families, while, in fact, right until *One from the Heart*, solitude is what has largely motivated him. The puppets fight it out as best they can. *Apocalypse Now* and *One from the Heart* are ultimately two sides of the same coin: the same *folie de grandeur*, the same cult of spectacle, whether on a large historical scale or a very small one. The films come in pairs, as if one is a corrective to its predecessor: *The Godfather* and *The Godfather Part II*, *Apocalypse Now* and *One from the Heart*, and then *The Outsiders* (1983) and *Rumble Fish* (1983). The domestic tone of *One from the Heart* is a corrective to *Apocalypse Now*, in that it speaks of the daily lives of Americans and tries to do something Coppola had never attempted before: to make a love story. Once again, he takes his inspiration from his own life, this time from his affair with his assistant Melissa Mathison during the shoot in the Philippines and the breakdown of his marriage. But Coppola's extravagance got the better of him.

He has never recovered from *One from the Heart*. The first screening, at Radio City Music Hall in January 1982, was a disaster, and rumour to that effect spread like wildfire. The sale of the studios was announced in April; the dream had lasted only a few months. The Zoetrope company continues to exist — it is Coppola's other, 'collective', name. But he had made a personal commitment to pay off his debts, and it took him ten years. At the same time, elsewhere, Michael Cimino was bleeding money with *Heaven's Gate* (1980) and Scorsese was getting out of his depth with *The King of Comedy* (1982). The years 1981 and 1982 marked the end of the most ambitious directors' dreams of independence, whereas Lucas and Spielberg were enjoying the rewards of being

Electronic cinema

'So where's Coppola, then?', wonders the visitor to the set of *One from the Heart*. The director's voice can be heard over the loudspeakers while he is shut in his booth, his eyes fixed on the monitors that show him what's happening on the set. He looks at the shot again, edits it with the previous one, compares it with another take. It all takes place in that silver van, the Silverfish, where the video viewing system is installed. Lording it over his Zoetrope studios, Coppola is experimenting with what he calls 'electronic cinema'.

Electronic cinema is first of all a way of going back to the drawing board, a *tabula rasa* that involves all aspects of cinema. Broadly speaking, it refers to the arrival of computers in the process of filmmaking, and there is no doubt that in this respect Coppola was ahead of his times. He was the first to foresee that digitization, virtual editing and the Internet would revolutionize the way things were done. At the 1979 Oscars ceremony, far from the steamy heat of the jungle, he announced himself the prophet of this new era, the Kurtz of electronic cinema.

Later, he was more specific: 'We're talking about a spatial system, not a linear one. When we make a film we work on it as a whole, even when it's only the germ of an idea. It's not a question any more of writing a screenplay and taking bits of it and then going through a post-production stage to bring them all together. The pre-production, production and post-production all take place at the same time' (*Cahiers du cinéma*, no. 334–335, April 1982, p.44). It's a hugely ambitious aim, and presupposes that Coppola's company, Zoetrope, has proper studios in which to combine all these stages, and a remuneration system for writers and actors, who will be available on demand, as in the heyday of the 'majors'. The technical revolution would paradoxically bring about a return to a particular concept of Hollywood. *One from the Heart* is its symbol and prototype in its form also, which celebrates the classic musical and uses visual effects inserted in novel ways. When his studio collapsed, Coppola had to adapt. The dream of 'doing it all' was abandoned, and with it, the attractions of an 'electronic aesthetic', in which actors crushed under the weight of technology would find themselves wandering through a giant videogame. From *The Outsiders* onward, Coppola has always been physically present on set with his actors. At the same time, his working method has changed for good, and is based on 'pre-visualization'.

This consists of three stages: 1. The director films the storyboard in video, creating a big 'strip cartoon'. 2. He then films in video the actors rehearsing against a blue background, onto which he can paste drawings or photos. In this way he obtains a preliminary shooting-script, which he fits together. 3. Lastly, for the shoot itself, he films in video, in a format larger than 35mm, so that he has the images immediately available and can assemble them and produce a first edit by the time the shoot is completed. This very curious procedure, in which the stages vary in length from film to film, is an aspect of Coppola's total control of the creation process.

People have criticized it, as if these films were no more than life-sized models, representing the mechanical execution of a programme that makes it possible to visualize a film before it is made. One might suspect that precisely the reverse is true: that it is an obsession with putting reality to the test. Distrust of the written word and of abstraction always leads Coppola to see what effect he is achieving. It's a concern shared by all those involved, since in this way everyone can see and judge very early on, and that affects what each person does (acting, special effects, sound, etc.). Technology or no technology, what we see here is the director's old theatrical training, with its rehearsals and run-throughs, to which he had always remained loyal.

pure entertainers, buoyed up by their joint success with *Raiders of the Lost Ark* (1981). Coppola was already elsewhere, in Tulsa, Oklahoma.

Rescued by youth

Many people think the break imposed by *One from the Heart* forced Coppola to make a series of contract movies in order to get back on his feet. That is not at all true of the next two films he made. He had set his heart on filming S. E. Hinton's debut novel, *The Outsiders*, before his flop had even been released, and while he was adapting it, he read and decided to film another of her novels, *Rumble Fish*. It all began in a strange way: a librarian had sent him a letter signed by students at her school, asking that he adapt their favourite book, *The Outsiders*, written by a sixteen-year-old in Tulsa in 1970. Coppola was touched. He read it and emerged from the Zoetrope studios rescued by youth. He signed the film with a simple 'Francis Coppola'. The film's first voice-over sentence has the ring of a new beginning: 'When I stepped out into the bright sunlight, from the darkness of the movie house, I had only two things on my mind: Paul Newman, and a ride home.' That's what *The Outsiders* is: a 'ride home', after a period of being a prisoner in the 'house of cinema'. *Rumble Fish*, made immediately afterwards, proved to be as exciting as the first two *Godfather* movies. One 'classic' film and another, 'experimental', one, shot in the same place, with the same team of people.

Following pages: Francis Ford Coppola with C. Thomas Howell (left) and Matt Dillon (right) on the set of *The Outsiders* (1983).

A Golden Age

The Outsiders is a wonder. And wonder is also the subject of the film. 'Stay gold', says the song over the title credits, written by Carmine Coppola and sung by Stevie Wonder. 'Stay gold' refers to the innocence of Ponyboy Curtis (played by C. Thomas Howell), an orphan raised by his two older brothers, and a member of a gang called the Greasers. The Greasers fight the Socials, or Socs, rich kids who are able to take their cars to the drive-in to pick up girls, while those without a cent have to slip under the wire fence and sit in a row out in the open. The Greasers have no family and no future; they're growing up together in a gang, doing the best they can.

In this random bunch of orphans, we can see, in a way, the family ethos of the *Godfather* movies, if only in the striking detail of their greased-down hair. But that is where the comparison ends; these kids don't just have no parents. Johnny, like Huckleberry Finn, sleeps on the street, barely keeping warm by wrapping himself in newspaper. When the most vulnerable of them, Johnny (Ralph Macchio), stabs one of the Socs to death while rescuing Ponyboy, the two boys hide out in the countryside on the advice of Dallas (Matt Dillon). The countryside is 'gold'. They live in a church, surrounded by animals, a racoon knocks on the window, and they read *Gone with the Wind*. Ponyboy dyes his hair blond in order to pass unnoticed, and it is as if gold had been poured over his head. It reminds one of Charles Laughton's *The Night of the Hunter* (1955) (for the suspended moment of the two boys' escape on the river), or Joseph Losey's *The Boy with Green Hair* (1949), the story of a boy who wakes up one morning with emerald-green hair. But in a surprising reversal, the youngsters, now joined by Dallas, find themselves prisoners in another house, just as dilapidated as their dream church, but a nightmare version of it: the boys enter a burning house to try to save a number of children trapped by the flames. An owl flies out in terror, and Johnny is crushed by a beam, crushed by his good intentions in rescuing the children (but it was worth it, he insists), and crushed most of all by so much gold (the setting sun, his blond hair, the flames), as if there was no way one could ever get over all that gold.

Coppola had said: '*One from the Heart* is a film about neon. The next one, *The Outsiders*, will be a film about sunset.'[21] It is a particular quality of light that links the two together. Sunset is clearly the end of childhood. The poem by Robert Frost, 'Nothing Gold Can Stay', has an echo in Elia Kazan's *Splendor in the Grass* (1961), in which Natalie Wood finds expressed in a line from Wordsworth the disenchantment that has filled her at losing 'the splendour in the grass, the glory in the flower'. The splendour in the grass is to be found everywhere in *The Outsiders*. Coppola is filming in the actual places described in the novel, in Tulsa, a choice that is the reverse of the confined quality of *One from the Heart*, and he pays particular attention to nature, not only in the rural interlude, but all the way through: the park where Johnny and Ponyboy are attacked by the Socs, the other one where Dallas falls under a hail of police bullets, and all the shots filmed from a distance, in which the silhouettes of the figures stand out against the horizon and the sunset.

But too little has been made of the fact that this nature is strangely artificial, surrounded by concrete or bathed in the exaggerated light of the setting sun. It is the profound originality of *The Outsiders* that it combines location shooting and studio shots, as if electronic cinema had seeped into this traditional, elegiac film. Ponyboy has a discussion with Cherry (Diane Lane), the girlfriend of the Socs' leader, with the horizon (or more accurately a back projection) behind them, as their hair is blown by the wind (or by a fan). The teenagers are enclosed in their time-bubble, encircled by the sunset; it has the artificial magic of classic Hollywood, of *Gone with the Wind*. The beauty is too beautiful, the sunset too dramatic, and the whole film is pervaded by the opening credits, in which an immense title glides electronically over the members of the gang as if over a series of dead bodies.[22] The artificiality of the rural setting, which is as fake as in *The Night of the Hunter*, places us in the distant, mythical past. It takes only dye to turn these blond heads into golden heads, and thus to go from nostalgia for one's youth in the 1960s to a general regret for a golden age.

Matt Dillon, C. Thomas Howell and Ralph Macchio in *The Outsiders* (1983).

Matt Dillon and Mickey Rourke in
Rumble Fish (1983).

The Outsiders (1983).

On its release, *The Outsiders* was criticized for being too traditional a film, riding the wave of nostalgia for the 1960s, begun by *American Graffiti*. However, just as *One from the Heart* placed itself in the tradition of the musical, so Coppola places himself in the tradition of the film about adolescence, which has become an American genre per se.[23] Within that genre, Coppola finds himself at an equal distance from traditional romanticism and the contemporary view of adolescence. He treats the adolescents less as rebels (in the James Dean tradition) than as big children. In this way he bridges the gap between Nicholas Ray and Larry Clark, who made *Kids* (1995) and *Wassup Rockers* (2006), and who also happened to have started out as a photographer in Tulsa in the 1960s. Dallas is still in the tradition of the rebel without a cause; Ponyboy and Johnny, on the other hand, are children. When Ponyboy comes back from the hospital, in a scene shot with great sensitivity, his elder brother picks up the sleeping boy in his arms and carries him into the house. Here Coppola, aged forty-three, whose eldest son Gian-Carlo, then nineteen, was his assistant, shows a delicate combination of nostalgia for his own youth and paternal affection.

The ticking clock and the rust in 'Rusty'

The clouds speed by, the hands of a clock turn every which way, and we hear the click of a time-switch: Coppola's next film, *Rumble Fish*, starts at breakneck speed, eclipsing the contemplative beauty of *The Outsiders*. The tone is set right from the start. The dialogue is very sharp, and the characters speak their lines over one another. The soundtrack is an unusual mix of drumming, mechanical clicks and heartbeats.

As Coppola has often said, the subject of *Rumble Fish* is time. The urgent time of the clock, the time of youth, passing so quickly, the lost time that the slow-witted Rusty — short for Russell — James (played by Matt Dillon) tries to make up, and the time that separates him from his older brother, Motorcycle Boy (played by Mickey Rourke), who lives too fast and dies too young. Is Rusty 'rusty', in the sense of being 'out of practice'? It's a paradox, because he has remained a child; it's Motorcycle Boy who is 'rusty', and he ceased to be a child at the age of five. He's only twenty-one, and already he's an old guy who has never been truly young, full of the world-weariness of someone who has lived for a thousand years.

'A new pinball machine', by Serge Daney

…To watch a Coppola film – and *Rumble Fish* more than all the rest put together – is like finding yourself examining a new pinball machine. A new-look Gottlieb, or a Bally (you hardly see the Williams any more), into whose slot, anxious and excited, you'll insert your old ten-franc coin. How does it work? Where are the bumpers, the lanes, the spinners, the targets, the captive or extra balls, the "special"? What kind of noise does it make? How do you win? …

His "style" consists in setting out – conspicuously if possible – the broad assumptions under which this or that detail (visual or auditory) is subsumed, so that it creates, as in jazz, a little solo. This is what he started doing in *One from the Heart*, something in between unnecessary exposition and last-minute verification, between a test and a check-up. So *Rumble Fish* contains "solos" in the cinematography (by Stephen H. Burum), in

the words, the music (by Stewart Copeland, the drummer with the Police), the gestures, the camera movements – everything. They refer to nothing else, unless it is the pleasure felt by someone revving up a very fine engine before putting it in gear and driving off …

["Rusty James"] are the words heard most frequently in the film. The hero is constantly being called by his name, sometimes as a challenge, sometimes with affection, often in the way we talk to a child to get it used to the idea that he has a name – his own name, which belongs to him and nobody else. That "Rusty James!", spoken with an Oklahoma accent (the film is set in Tulsa), is a way of winning the audience's loyalty, like the "Try me again" on the Xenon pinball machine. There are many other examples of this art of amplification. They include the decision to film in black and white, on the grounds that the Motorcycle Boy

doesn't see colours, or the long scene between the two brothers, in which the elder one (the Boy in question) incessantly asks the younger one a single question: "Why?", to which the other one finally bursts out, "Why why?" And the scene goes on, stuck on this little word as if it were a clot of blood.

In this way, F. "Ford" C. creates, laboriously, today's "mannerist" cinema. This Italian-American is our Parmesan or our Primatice … The mistake would be to think that Coppola is simply content to add his hypertrophied style to themes that are in the end pretty much worn out. That is not entirely true.

The man has a "world view" that fits perfectly with the chaos and confusion he is trying to impose on cinema … Motorcycle Boy is in the (highly "Coppolian") situation of someone who has gone to the limit, has found nothing there, and for want of anything better to do, cultivates the look of a rather

taciturn dandy (and it turns out he's not only colour-blind, but half deaf, too!). …

It is clear that *Rumble Fish* is the story of lost illusions. Embodied in human form, the ideal lets us down. When they are idolized, the stars take a fall (remember Kurtz/Brando, in *Apocalypse Now*). That's no more than is to be expected. A film director who wants to rethink the power of illusion in the cinema needs to believe that the world (the "real" world) is itself an illusion. That it is made up of appearances, winks of God's eye and false truisms on earth … At bottom, the world barely exists. Coppola only works its material to regain a little of its soul.

This is an extract from the article 'Rusty James' (the French title of *Rumble Fish*), published in *Libération*, 15 February 1984.

Matt Dillon and Mickey Rourke in *Rumble Fish* (1983).

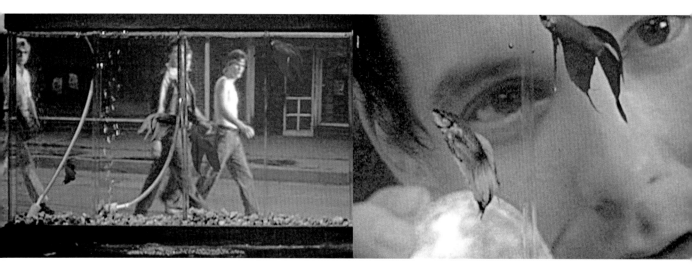

Rumble Fish is the story of an infatuation, that of the 'warm' Rusty, the gang-leader, with the 'cool' Motorcycle Boy, the ex-leader of a gang who's now going straight and who returns to his old neighbourhood after a trip to California. The 'ghost' has an aura around him: he poses like James Dean in the magazines, and speaks in a low voice as if he has left everything behind him. This infatuation really existed, it was Francis Coppola's for his older brother,[24] once a gang member, whose period leather jacket is worn in the film by his own son, Nicolas Cage, in the minor role of an Iago figure.

Rumble Fish is the visual story of another infatuation, this time with the old Hollywood that Coppola, its heir, revives with a cheeky magnificence. The use of black and white, the short-focus lens, the fragmentation, the shadows on the walls, the smoke machine, the voices echoing in empty space: all this makes us think of Orson Welles. Coppola dipped into the 1940s to make his film noir, into the 1960s to portray adolescent rebellion.[25]

From the purely 'audiovisual' point of view, this is Coppola's most accomplished work. The composer, Stewart Copeland, the drummer with the Police, juggles with sounds. This stylization is paralleled in the character's distorted perception. Motorcycle Boy is colour-blind and half deaf, he speaks in a whisper and visualizes his own utterances 'like a black-and-white TV with the sound turned low.' The hallucinatory walk along a studio street, among soldiers and prostitutes, recalls the sensory confusion of *Apocalypse Now*. It's a kind of knowing allegory: the red Siamese fighting fish that symbolize the aggressive teenagers (rumble fish = 'fighting fish') emerge in colour from the black and white. Coppola has said that he was trying to

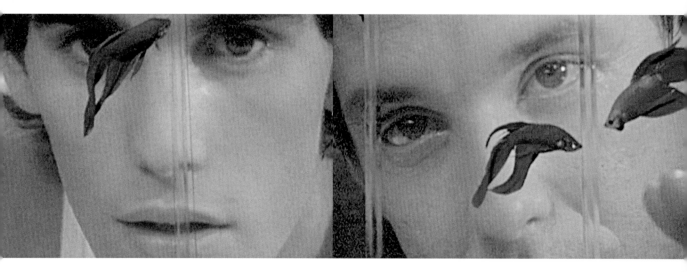

make an 'art film for teenagers'. There's nothing dry about it, however, and it is unusually sensual: Matt Dillon and Diane Lane (playing Patty, his girl-friend) intertwine their bare arms, and Dillon, with his headband and tee-shirt, became a sex-icon.

Once again, it is all tinged with myth. The graffiti on the walls recall the glory of the dethroned king: 'The Motorcycle Boy reigns.' Not 'rules' but 'reigns, because we're talking about royalty. Later on, someone says of him, 'He's royalty in exile.' As in *The Godfather* and *Apocalypse Now*, a man has wished to be king. King of a neighbourhood — that isn't saying much, but the dandy on the motorcycle acts like a Shakespearean tragic hero. Motorcycle Boy is in exile in his own turf. Because he has no more orders to give, he has become a hollow man. In the pool hall, Mickey Rourke strikes a wistful pose, with his hand against his face, like the one that punctuates *The Godfather Part II*. The king has no stature, he is rather, according to Coppola, a 'French intellectual' in the style of Camus. Certainly the French-style jacket he wears (out of place among these tough guys) turns him into a 'stranger'.

Rumble Fish was very influential.[26] It is quite moving to listen to the commentary on the DVD because Coppola is describing the only moment in his career when he felt completely fulfilled. The shoot went without a hitch, using actors with whom he had worked before and who had the mak-ings of a company, his experimentation created a perfect artificial world, and the subject (his rela-tionship with his brother) was close to his heart. He is self-critical about having been too versatile at the time: why try to demonstrate that you can do everything, when you should only do the things you desperately want to?

Mickey Rourke in *Rumble Fish* (1983).

Rear-view cinema

There's no question but that when Coppola said that, he was thinking of the disaster of *The Cotton Club*. The failure of *Rumble Fish* (its receipts in the United States were $2.5 million — a mere one-tenth those of *The Outsiders*) put him in a delicate situation, and he accepted a commission from a producer he knew well: Robert Evans, who had produced *The Godfather* — not his happiest professional experience. The ground was all the shakier because Evans had intended to make *The Cotton Club* himself and, for want of other alternatives, tried to recreate the dream team of *the Godfather* (Mario Puzo wrote the screenplay). When Coppola arrived on the scene, the film was already a financial black hole.

It was clearly an embarrassment for Coppola when he came to deal with the life of *The Cotton Club*, a famous night-club of the 1930s, where blacks danced, but whites drank, all with a 'Mafia' flavour. Its relationship with *The Godfather* is similar to that of *The Outsiders* with *Rumble Fish*: the transition from a sober classicism to a fast-moving stylization, from the recreation of a mythic story to its fragmentation. Between the making of the two films, experimentation in electronic cinema had become much more complex. The stylistic repertory (several brief shots in quick succession, close-ups, high- and low-angle shots and a short-focus lens) makes *The Cotton Club* a negative film, like a rebellious son who has created the biggest possible trouble in order to get out from under his father's shadow.

Without looking any further, Coppola simply adopted Puzo's screenplay. He took little trouble over the story, and the characters are reduced to nothing more than cardboard cut-outs. He is in his element when dealing with an innocent's initiation into evil (as in *Apocalypse Now*) or the adult world (in *Rumble Fish*), but *The Cotton Club* is his first cynical film. The hero, Dixie Dwyer (played by Richard Gere), is indifferent to everything, from the first shot to the last; he has nothing to learn. The subject could have been a beautiful one: Dixie is being paid by a gangster to take care of his mistress (played by Diane Lane) and falls in love with her. A story of love between

The Cotton Club (1984).

two lost whores? Coppola doesn't think so. Dixie becomes a ham actor, imitating in Hollywood the gestures favoured by gangsters, such as the puppet crooner whose strings are pulled by the Don at the beginning of *The Godfather*.

In his customary way, Coppola adapts his style to his subject. This volatile world is superficially drawn, and these pathetic figures crudely represented. The only ones to be 'saved' are the blacks, but their parts were cut in the edit (the last straw?) and they are reduced to so many dancing shadows. Coppola achieves some brilliant things, like the patter of a tap-dancer's feet in time to machine-gun fire, and he adapts his own brisk pace to the rhythms of the jazz age. But the idea of a stage, which has always been crucial for him and comes from his training in the theatre, is absent here. The camera films in the midst of the dancers, who ignore the lights; the characters are trapped in the background, like insects between the slats of a Venetian blind. They have no time to pose or to speak; if they do speak, it's during a night of love devoid of desire. The visual treatment is dazzling but the picture it depicts is no more than that, it has no heart.

Two people reconciled

Ever since the disaster of *One from the Heart*, Coppola had been forced to accept commissions: 'Rip Van Winkle' (1985),[27] a fifty-minute television film for HBO, and a short for Michael Jackson, *Captain Eo*, lasting seventeen minutes, at $1 million a minute. In particular, he agreed to make a fantasy film, *Peggy Sue Got Married* (1986), which the critics found 'impersonal'. He accepted it because of the $3 million fee, which enabled him to save the Sentinel Building, Zoetrope's headquarters. But while he was waiting for his lead actress, Kathleen Turner, to extricate herself from her previous contract, he had plenty of time to take over the script and turn a light comedy into a bitter treatment of the passage of time.

It's the story of a forty-something woman, who, in a bizarre time-switch, finds she is a teenager again. The light-handed direction, the fact that it was a 'college movie', and came out soon after Robert Zemeckis's *Back to the Future* (1985), all masked the originality of what Coppola was trying to do. *Peggy Sue Got Married* chimes with the two 'Tulsa' films, which were still fresh in the memory: nostalgia for youth, when time stands still (in *The Outsiders*), and the accelerated loss of innocence (in *Rumble Fish*). *Peggy Sue Got Married* even resonates more distantly with the juxtaposition of the two epochs in *The Godfather Part II*. This small film reveals the core theme of Coppola's work, time: how we age, but how we are rejuvenated, too; how we lose our youth, and how we find it again. It could have been called *Youth Without Youth*.

The young woman 'without youth', Peggy Sue, finds herself face to face with her mother, whom she is moved to see ('Mom, I forgot you were ever this young'), and with her little sister and her dead grandparents. After hearing her grandmother's voice, she explains to her mother why she is crying: 'I dreamed that Grandma died.' The journey is all about the family, a journey back to the one you knew only as a child, and of which your memories have faded. It's an impossible fantasy, but one in which Coppola firmly believes, that you can meet your parents when they're the same age as you. Peggy Sue takes a deep breath and sings the national anthem for all she's worth, because this time she will enjoy these moments of happiness to the full.

Peggy Sue goes back to make peace with herself. When the film begins, she's dressed as a prom queen, and she is meeting her old friends at a high-school reunion. She's in the process of getting a divorce from Charlie (Nicolas Cage), the class rebel, to whom she has been married since high school. In her life 'through the looking-glass', she rejects Charlie, who is childish and indecisive; she is determined not to make the same mistake twice, and indulges her old fantasy of sleeping with the broodingly handsome Michael. But she is touched by Charlie's failings, and says, 'What am I going to do with you?', as if after all she is stuck with him; for his part, the handsome kid is still just a kid, with his high-flown quotations from Kerouac and his fantasy of living a simple life in the country. The magical tour de force of *Peggy Sue Got Married* is that it makes us accept this comedy of remarriage without bitterness or naiveté. Peggy

Sue makes a 'new life' in another sense, when she says: this is my life, Charlie is my husband, and I wouldn't change them for all the world. She makes peace with herself. It is not a matter of being resigned but of accepting her fate. The American myth of the second chance clashes with this certainty, expressed in the past tense: Peggy Sue got married. She got married, and she can go wherever she likes, but this bond is indissoluble.

At the end of the film, Peggy Sue invites Charlie to come over and eat strudel, a reminder of a word that has occurred before: 'It's my Grandma's strudel that's kept this family together.' And it's also a reminder of another 'cake', from the beginning of Coppola's career. The final credits of *You're a Big Boy Now* make a single motif of the teenage couple who have fallen for one another and the double twist of a pretzel as it is being made.

Self-portraits in black and pink

Gardens of Stone (1987) pursues the theme of time and the generation gap. It's 1968, and Sergeant Hazard (James Caan), member of the honour guard at Arlington National Cemetery, befriends the son of one of his old comrades-in-arms and tries to tell him what he needs to do if he is to survive in Vietnam. So here we are, back in the 1960s again, and the Vietnam War, even if the battlefront stays off-screen. (As Hazard says, 'There's no front line in Vietnam.') But these are dark times: in 1968, Hazard is already a veteran. He sees his younger self in Willow, as if the two of them were the same man at two stages in his life: before and after. Cheeky, innocent and sassy; bent, disappointed and awkward: the two ages that interest Coppola most are brought together in the uneasy encounter between the one who has returned and the one who is eager to go.

This encounter of gold and rust creates a father—son bond between the two men. It is a bond cut short after the first scenes, since Coppola alters the 'coming-of-age' novel by having Willow die. His coffin is brought back from Vietnam to be buried at Arlington, the 'stone garden' of which Hazard is the pathetic guardian. It is a difficult image to watch when you know of the tragic event

Kabuki cinema

'I have been studying Japanese theatre for several years, and it has been a big influence. It's a form of theatre in which set design, music, dance and song carry the plot in turn and are brought into the spotlight one after the other to tell the story at a particular moment … The instrumentalists in a jazz orchestra do the same thing: the trumpet-player gets up and plays a solo, the drummer follows him, and so on. In *One from the Heart* the various elements are treated in the same way.'

This is an extract from an interview, published in *Positif*, no. 262, April 1982.

'What interested me [*in Gardens of Stone*] were the emotions associated with military ritual; in my mind, that was the subject of the film. But when I saw it in a theatre, I noticed that the audience didn't respond to it in the same way. It was the same problem as with the songs in *One from the Heart*; the audience refused to transpose ritual to the level of feeling, and wanted me to do it for them. That's where the difference lies: I want the audience to make the synthesis so that they feel the emotion … That's the big problem: how to communicate an emotion to the audience? Of course, there's the method based on the dramatic structure of the scene, which consists of filming the faces and bringing out the emotion through the dramatic conflict. The audience members know that and accept it because they know when they should feel sad and when they should feel happy. I've always thought there should be other ways of expressing emotion, as, for example, the way it's done in Japanese theatre. To my way of thinking, emotion should come from the music, the images, the composition, everything combined into one; it shouldn't come only from the actors.'

This is an extract from an interview, published in *Cahiers du cinéma*, no. 415, January 1989.

Opposite page: D. B. Sweeney in *Gardens of Stone* (1987).

Above: Francis Ford Coppola on the set of *Gardens of Stone* (1987).

Jeff Bridges in *Tucker: A Man and His Dream* (1988).

that had just occurred in Coppola's life. While the film was being shot, his elder son, Gian-Carlo, with whom he had worked very closely, died in a speedboat accident at the age of twenty-three. It was a cruel irony that the fictional death of a son should find an echo in the director's private life.

Gardens of Stone presents itself as a film about Vietnam without Vietnam, the opposite of *Platoon* and *Full Metal Jacket*, which were released within the same six-month period. And yet the screen is full of deafening images of the war. First of all, following the credit sequence in the cemetery, we hear the noise of a helicopter picking up soldiers exposed to danger, an obvious reminder of *Apocalypse Now*. Next, the war is omnipresent on the screens of the television sets that are always on in the background; we know the war was broadcast uncensored and that it infiltrated people's homes with unprecedented violence. Lastly, there is the sudden transition from the scene of Willow's wedding to full-screen TV images showing anonymous, disoriented soldiers. Vietnam haunts the film to the point where it blows the image apart, before disappearing discreetly off-screen.

The clasped hands of two soldiers in the images of war that we briefly glimpse, the clasped hands of Willow's widow and Hazard's future wife at the funeral are sufficient indication of emotions that are too powerful to be dramatized. Coppola shoots in a classic, traditional fashion, he does not use any visual tricks. As usual, like a chameleon, he adapts his style to his subject.

That has never been more true than in *Tucker: The Man and His Dream* (1988), the epic of a small automobile designer in competition with the Detroit big shots at the end of World War II. *Gardens of Stone* had the cold look of a tomb, its shots aligned like rows of crosses. *Tucker* is like the fast, comfortable car, full of revolutionary features, which its designer wishes to sell to the American public under the noses of the big guys. The film is a long promotional piece for this open tourer, the Tucker Torpedo, and it steals the aesthetic of advertising. A 'gadget' film, if you like, that stuns you with its speed and Vittorio Storaro's flashy lighting (he was the cinematographer on *One from the Heart*).

The project was an old one. As a child, Francis had eagerly awaited the launch of the Torpedo, but the major manufacturers got the better of the small entrepreneur and he was able to make only fifty of them. When he grew up, Coppola bought one, and after completing *Apocalypse Now* he tried without success to make a bio-pic in the form of a musical in a sombre key. In 1985, George Lucas offered to produce it, on condition that it was neither a musical nor sombre. Once again, Coppola found himself under a number of obligations, first to Lucasfilm, which set the overall tone, that of an optimistic hymn to America with a feel-good ending typical of Spielberg–Lucas productions, and then to the Tucker family, who asked that he give a truthful account of their celebrity ... apart from his extramarital affair.

It seems a long way from the pride of the wunderkind, hoping to have the establishment bowing down before him. And yet his films have never reflected him so closely, whether through force of circumstances, as in *Gardens of Stone*, or through obstinacy and perseverance. *Tucker* is clearly a self-portrait. Tucker builds his factory in Chicago, near the power base of Detroit, in the same way as Coppola set up Zoetrope in San Francisco, not far from Hollywood. Tucker naively believes he's going to bring down the establishment, that his team of family and friends will win out against the power of big money, and that his brilliant prototype will be the beginning of a whole new ball game. It's like a picture in miniature of what Coppola had gone through in a decade, including his private life.[28] We should look kindly on that difficult decade. In his sudden fall from grace, he gained in humility, and learned how to work with other people again. *Apocalypse Now* and *One from the Heart* together represent an interlude of autarchy, when he imagined he was a dictator. From *The Outsiders* on, he had to learn to work *with* a writer, and *for* a school. He embraced the practice of dedicating his films; he was making films for somebody, and for a studio, too. Films made under the name 'Francis Coppola'.[29]

Top: Francis Ford Coppola with Sofia Coppola on the set of *Life Without Zoe*, the second segment of *New York Stories* (1989).

Bottom: Francis Ford Coppola, Woody Allen and Martin Scorsese, the *New York Stories* directors (1989).

Good Sense

**From *The Godfather Part III*
to *The Rainmaker***

Sofia Coppola and Andy Garcia in
The Godfather Part III (1990).

Where did Coppola stand at the end of the 1980s? A series of films made rapidly one after the other, including three irrevocable failures (*Rumble Fish, The Cotton Club* and *Gardens of Stone*), a decade framed by a professional debacle (*One from the Heart*) and a family tragedy. He launched into an extravagant project, *Megalopolis*, which would occupy him for over ten years without being completed. In the meantime, he took on more commissions. The first, a short entitled *Life Without Zoe*, one of the three segments of *New York Stories* (1989), was a frivolous story, written with his daughter Sofia, about the life of a rich young girl living in one of New York's grand hotels. Following this 'home movie', made for his daughter and a forerunner of her film *Lost in Translation* (2003), Coppola finally agreed to shoot, in New York and Italy, a third *Godfather* film.

Black ochre

Coppola had long resisted the idea of closing up *The Godfather* with a third part. When he agreed to do so, he intended to make 'a film in the style of *The Godfather*', and yet *The Godfather Part III* (1990) is in no way a reprise of the other two. Coppola discards the gloomy solemnity and the use of long shots for a closer, more intimate style of filming.

Opposite page: Andy Garcia and Al Pacino in
The Godfather Part III (1990).

Above: Sofia Coppola, Diane Keaton, Al Pacino, John Savage,
Andy Garcia and Talia Shire in *The Godfather Part III* (1990).

In the first two parts interest was divided between several characters, while this one concentrates on Michael. That decision, partly due to the defection of Robert Duvall (who demanded to be paid the same amount as Al Pacino), excluded a summit meeting of the two 'sons', Michael Corleone and Tom Hagen. But it enabled Coppola, in the absence of the theme of family conflict, to delve into Michael's inner 'empire'.

The film opens with the Nevada property in ruins. Michael has come back to live in New York, alone, he is tired and psychologically wounded. He hasn't seen his children for eight years, but how can he be so old? There is nothing in the visuals to suggest the date of the action (1979), and no period details. Gordon Willis's orange-browns, very different from the yellowish blacks of the first two parts, do not chime with the atmosphere of mental decline. We are in a 'time afterwards'. Coppola has said that he saw the film 'less as a third part than as an epilogue.'

Its subject is redemption, first of all on the social level: Michael wishes to repair his position vis-à-vis the Church and to put his illicit business affairs in order. Ironically, the 'godfather' is decorated by the Pope, as if each were the mirror image of the other (at the end of *The Godfather*, people kiss the Don's hand as they do that of His Holiness in Rome). In a further irony, the family makes up the shameful deficits of the Vatican Bank. At the very moment when Michael attempts to 'convert' (economically speaking) to legal business, he realizes that corruption reaches the highest places of all. Even the papacy's money is dirty. Michael closes his accounts with his former partners, so that he can leave the Mafia, but the Five Families do not agree to it. Caught between the fire from his corrupt ex-associates and the cynical Swiss bankers, Michael finds it impossible to make his conversion.

Once again, the deeper question is a moral one. The sharp criticism of a thoroughly rotten system shows how the *Godfather* films become increasingly politicized as we ascend the ladder of power. Nevertheless, the film's heart is elsewhere. Michael suffers crises brought on by his diabetes, in which he shouts the name of Fredo, the brother he murdered; he weeps as he makes his confession in Rome. He's no longer the same man; eaten away by remorse, he begs for redemption. This third part makes the trilogy turn back on itself. Following a pattern that Coppola calls 'ABA', the third part takes up again the themes of the first (the ageing Don, the question of the succession) except that this time the Godfather does not look back on his life with satisfaction, on his deathbed, but weeps at the debacle that he himself has brought about.

And what remains of the succession? Three children will each represent a possible heir, or an idea, like the four sons in *The Godfather*. The first is a newcomer, Vincent (Andy Garcia), Sonny's illegitimate son. He's a 'mad dog', who makes the old Godfather apoplectic, but is very quickly welcomed into the family circle. Boastful Vincent awakens the old Don. Pacino gives a start in his chair at the first example of eccentricity, as if electrified and brought to life. As in *Gardens of Stone*, time 'after' runs in parallel with time 'before': an old man bonds with a young one, who has come to drive him off the scene. The succession is assured.

Then there's the daughter, Mary, played by Coppola's daughter, Sofia.[30] Mary is innocent, and admires her father, who returns her love ('I would burn in hell to keep you safe'), but the screenplay sacrifices her in two respects. She falls in love with her cousin Vincent, a forbidden love that would almost guarantee infertility in a degenerate family; and she dies for the sins of the family, struck by the bullet intended for her father. Coppola originally thought of making a film called *The Death of Michael Corleone*, in which he had the brilliant idea of letting Michael burn in hell and of having her die.

Mary's death is perhaps the most touching moment in all of Coppola's cinema. She falls down in a deathly silence, and just breathes the word 'Dad'. Kay draws back, screaming with pain, and

Francis Ford Coppola with Sofia Coppola on the set of *The Godfather Part III* (1990).

Michael howls, dazed, but the sound of his voice is delayed, as if it were coming from so far away that it takes a few seconds to reach us. Then it pierces the silence. It's a heartbreaking moment of total grief, encompassing Coppola's grief at losing his son while he was making *Gardens of Stone*, a death that his own daughter is re-enacting before his eyes. There is something new here: Coppola has found what was missing, a way of concluding the saga.

And lastly, there's the son, who is an opera singer, a profession that takes him out of the ambience of crime. Michael believes as deeply as Coppola in this sublimation through art. The last forty-five minutes are an apotheosis in which a number of crimes follow one another against a background of Mascagni's *Cavalleria rusticana*. For the last time, Michael orders his men to make a combined attack, which from beginning to end is under the cover of his son's singing. Coming out of the theatre, Michael lets it be known that

Al Pacino in *The Godfather Part III* (1990).

the Corleone family will henceforth speak with a single voice, a few seconds before he loses his own in the face of his daughter's death. Everything passes. Only art is eternal.

The three *Godfather* films are the cornerstones of Coppola's work, and they have it all: the family saga, the *folie de grandeur*, the meaning of time, melancholia. The trilogy stands up miraculously, when one considers that it was built gradually, with successive additions. The end of *The Godfather Part III* recapitulates moments of dancing: Michael and his daughter, Michael and his

first, Sicilian wife, Michael and Kay. The trilogy is a waltz in which melancholy holds up the action, and vanity makes each person's vanities crumble away. After the dance, Michael is framed sitting on a chair, somewhere in Sicily. He is made up, wearing an old hat: he's an old man. There's no title to say so, but ten years at least have passed. Are we now in the time of the narration itself, the present — 1990, perhaps? The Don is alone, as he was at the end of *The Godfather Part II*, but filmed from a distance, set apart, already dead. He falls off his chair without a sound.

Brando, Pacino, De Niro

The Godfather trilogy is a work on a grand scale. Coppola recalls how, before he started shooting the first part, he got all the actors to sit at a table with Marlon Brando and eat a meal. Brando, a key figure from the Actors Studio (the New York acting school set up by Elia Kazan in 1947 and headed by Lee Strasberg) was their 'godfather' in the art of performance. Coppola has also often described the metamorphosis undergone by Brando, who was dumbfounded when he suggested he do a make-up test; he put paper tissues in his mouth, to make himself look like a bulldog, put on a hoarse voice, chewed, mumbled and transformed himself into an old Sicilian. The projecting jaw, the creased forehead and the heavy make-up gave him a bundle of mannerisms that didn't care if it was grotesque. Even the props were grabbed in passing; it was enough for Coppola to throw a cat into Brando's lap just before the take, and it would be handled with great gentleness by an actor whose hands, mouth, eyes and neck were in constant whirling motion. The way he gently rubs his cheek with the back of his fingertips has gone down to posterity.

It is exciting to see the master's two disciples, Al Pacino and Robert De Niro, make their appearance on screen. But it would take all Coppola's powers of persuasion to get Paramount to accept them, such an unlikely choice at that date were these 'bad boys' from Little Italy, who were about to revolutionize the art of acting.

A direct descendant of Brando, De Niro plays the young Don in *The Godfather Part II*. He copies his elder's striking gestures and imitates his voice, without falling into mere mimicry, and his slender figure contrasts with the Don's heavy make-up. He takes the character in the direction of a cunning reserve, like a fox walking over the roof, or a slightly remote sphinx.

But the big excitement, of course, is Pacino. In *The Godfather* he is the essence of pure concentration, with his dark, level gaze, looking straight through the person he is speaking to and staring into the far distance – an inward gaze focused on his own destiny alone. His calm features mask and control his extreme tension (think of the restless movement of his eyes before he commits his first murder) and when he puts his thoughts into action, Pacino, a dancer as well as an actor, releases his innate gracefulness, as in the way he drops the revolver after the murder, or pushes Kay into the car and shuts the door. Pacino's performance is as if choreographed; he glides, moves seamlessly. Brando and De Niro are jerkier in their movements. When he returns in *The Godfather Part III*, fifteen years later, he is hardly recognizable, with his grey crew cut and dark glasses. He is all lassitude, incredibly stooped under the weight of his sins and his years. Pacino, who would shortly afterwards make a film about Richard III (*Looking for Richard*, 1996), has his sights set on Shakespeare. And on Brando, whose expressionistic style he emulates, but in a drier vein, with less grandiloquence and less irony. He is losing his concentrated energy, and his patience, and the Don's body, undermined by diabetes, is subject to sudden outbursts of violence. The broken puppet may fall to the ground at any moment.

Coppola has said that he hardly had to direct his three actors. One may doubt that when one learns how many times he made Pacino rehearse, as much in order to persuade the studios to hire the unknown actor as to allow his performance to 'settle'. But it is true that these three actors already had their family, even though it was a scattered one. Pacino suggested to his former teacher, Lee Strasberg, that he should play a minor role, that of his rival Hyman Roth, in The *Godfather Part II*. The family secret of the trilogy was the Actors Studio.

Opposite page, top: Marlon Brando in *The Godfather* (1972).

Opposite page, bottom: Al Pacino in *The Godfather Part II* (1974).

Right: Robert De Niro in *The Godfather Part II* (1974).

The balance sheet

Following that high note, Coppola had three successes in a row, one of which, *Bram Stoker's Dracula* (1992), was a triumph. The downward spiral of failure was a bad memory. Professionally speaking, the 1990s were the opposite of the 1980s. Coppola's versatility seemed to be turning into opportunism: in succession he shot a film about vampires, a fairy story for children and an adaptation of a work by a best-selling novelist. And yet it would be too easy to see in all of this a wild director tamed.

Dracula is part of an overall decorative lineage whose high points are *One from the Heart*, *The Cotton Club* and *Tucker*. Coppola even slaked his thirst for the Gothic vein, a thread that had led from the castle in *Dementia 13* to the house at Lake Tahoe in *The Godfather Part II* and the French plantation in *Apocalypse Now Redux*.[31] Here the individual, swallowed up by the setting (by Garrett Lewis) and drowning in his costumes (by the Japanese designer Eiko Ishioka), is reduced to a lengthening shadow or a ghoul climbing over endless walls. Far from the icy rigidity that is the usual demeanour of Count Dracula, here the beast spreads its evil power by the extension of its body into the setting. The editing brings together similar motifs (blood, shadows, circles), steering the metamorphoses of the vampire and the film in a screen continuity that aspires to the eternal.

Once again, Coppola is moved by the caprices of time. The vampire, both old and young, is a paradox over which Don Corleone's shadow moves. When he exclaims, 'I am the last of my kind!', we hear, word for word, the disillusioned soldiers of *Gardens of Stone*. On the other hand, in its other aspect, the story of love beyond death, the great romantic film, *Dracula* marks a weak point. And yet the story is driven by the quest for love: Count Dracula (the aptly named Gary Oldman, half seducer, half monster) re-encounters his wife (once more played by Winona Ryder) across a gap of several centuries. But, as in *One from the Heart*, its romanticism is unbalanced by its gigantism. Love stories will always be like an empty centre in Coppola's work. It is astonishing that at this point he should not be a director of films about love; marriage, yes, and the miseries of a woman in the orbit of a great man (*The Godfather*), but there's no romanticism there.

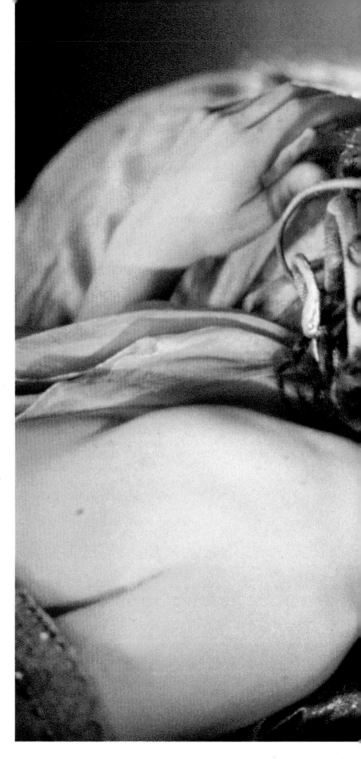

Michaela Bercu, Florina Kendrick, Monica Bellucci and
Keanu Reeves in *Bram Stoker's Dracula* (1992).

Francis Ford Coppola with Gary Oldman on the set of *Bram Stoker's Dracula* (1992).

Opposite page: Winona Ryder and Gary Oldman in *Bram Stoker's Dracula* (1992).

What he enjoys here (and he has a real field day with his son Roman, who was responsible for visual effects) is recreating the production conditions of a classic genre film, with a resourceful use of such things as back projections and make-up. *Dracula* resists the digital technology that was being introduced at the time, a paradox for a director who is normally a great enthusiast for it. But that's the whole appeal of his films: right from *One from the Heart* he had fantasized about filming his story 'live', unedited; here he imposes on himself the constraint of finding old-fashioned solutions, in order to recover the magic of the vampire movies he had consumed when he was young. The huge success of *Dracula* (it took $200 million worldwide) enabled Coppola to pay off the debt he had accumulated with *One from the Heart*. After making nine films in ten years, he could finally take a rest. He produced Kenneth Branagh's *Frankenstein* (1994) in the same baroque vein, but as for himself, he decided to take a back seat. In fact, he made two films set in the present day, something he had not done since *One from the Heart*; you have to go back to *The Conversation*, twenty years earlier, to see contemporary streets in a Coppola film. An amazing

feat: his whole oeuvre is, as it were, made backwards, the story is told facing the past.

When Disney offered *Jack* (1996) to Coppola, he immediately saw a personal resonance in it. This story of a child who lives in seclusion because he is ageing four times faster than normal (at the age of ten, he looks forty) reminded him of the year he spent in bed as a child with polio. More broadly, this film for children that apparently has nothing 'Coppolian' about it ties in with one of his obsessions: the relationship between people of different ages. One may think of *Peggy Sue* and the blurring of time in the *Godfather* films.[32] Robin Williams puts himself into the skin of a ten-year-old, before ending up in the make-up of a man of sixty-eight, while Diane Lane, who plays Jack's mother from his birth until he is seventeen, doesn't change at all. The emotion, which is real, springs from all these transformations that have to do with age.[33]

For the rest, *Jack* is for children, and doesn't claim to be anything more. The contract was fulfilled without fuss. The final shot shows Jack as a baby, just as the final image of *Tucker* showed us the designer as a child, on his bike. The return to childhood has become increasingly urgent. *Tucker* was dedicated to Coppola's son, Gio. *Jack* is dedicated to his granddaughter, Gia.

Coppola's films have always been fables. With *Jack* and *The Rainmaker* (1997), the plot devices are more obvious, but also lighter. *The Rainmaker*, adapted from a novel by John Grisham,[34] is the late flowering of a fable in the style of Frank Capra: the lone individual fighting the system, as in *Mr. Smith Goes to Washington* (1939).

A novice lawyer fights a powerful insurance company that is refusing to insure a young man with leukaemia. He wins so resounding a victory that the company goes bankrupt and is unable to pay up. We see pass before our eyes a deft summary of the great moments of Hollywood courtroom pleading. Matt Damon has James Stewart's clear gaze, and his amusing collaboration with a failed lawyer (Danny DeVito) gives this disillusioned story an element of comedy.

But beneath its modest surface, the film is exaggeratedly stylized: the use of a short focus lens, CinemaScope and high- and low-angle shots give it a larger-than-life look that suits the edifying fable. Coppola, who has never been in the habit of

treading carefully, moves easily from farce to melodrama (the lawyer falls in love with an abused wife) and the actors give it all they've got. The sharks of the financial and legal worlds are the new vampires; the idealist is a young man full of passion, who, like Tucker and Vincent in *The Godfather Part III*, is here to overthrow the powerful.

In the course of one shot, and in CinemaScope, Coppola slips a marionnette into the young patient's bed. In the same way as it does for Michael Corleone, an unwitting puppet manipulated by his father and his heritage, a son's sacrifice comes at a heavy price. Coppola sees it all with a kindly, but at the same time ironic, eye. And a wise one? As if powered by a calm strength, he seems to have withdrawn from the world, and to be filming youth, with its enduring faith, from a distance.

It would be impossible to understand this journey through Dracula, Disney and Capra (a journey that was never predictable) without revealing its inverse, *Megalopolis*, for which preparations were made in the greatest secrecy. In 2002, it was announced at a press conference in Marrakech that about sixty hours of film had been shot and were being edited. The film was described as an 'epic of contemporary life', in the mould of *One from the Heart*, an 'optimistic utopia' intended for his grandchildren. And then nothing — the project was abandoned.

Apart from that, Coppola spent part of his time at his renowned vineyard in Napa Valley, and part of it assisting with the production of his family's films[35]. He gave a lot of thought and attention to his own oeuvre, and to the DVD editions of his films, which were now issued with the addition of fascinating commentaries (the boxed set of *The Godfather* in particular), as well as promoting *Apocalypse Now Redux*, presented at Cannes in 2001. Then, at the point at which he seemed to have passed the baton on to others, he returned with a film shot in Romania: *Youth Without Youth* (2007). As with *The Outsiders*, youth was the escape route.

Left, top: Robin Williams in *Jack* (1996).

Left, bottom: Brian Kerwin and Robin Williams in *Jack* (1996).

A leap into eternity

With one leap in his four-league trainers, Jack, the child who is ageing too fast, is in the autumn of his life. He's seventeen years old, but his body is nearly seventy. His feet, wearing the red shoes from *The Wizard of Oz*, are still aged ten. It's graduation day, and his friends are celebrating the end of school. They have their lives ahead of them. But where are we,

actually? Coppola and his set designer, Dean Tavoularis, have done something brilliant: the ceremony takes place in the open air above a valley, with a distant village on a ridge, like a timeless city. It's the simulacrum of a heavenly agora; we have passed into eternity. Jack makes a valedictory speech, which has the ring of a profession of faith by Coppola – 'Make your

life spectacular' – all the more valid since the beret so often worn by Coppola now appears on Bill Cosby's head. Suddenly, all it takes is a back-lit view for us to make another leap across the years. In this final shot, how old is Jack? We're blinded by the sun; under the make-up and the light, his face disappears.

In the final credits, Jack becomes

again the ageless child he has always been. From a planetary perspective, death follows life in the blink of an eye, and vice versa. But the importance lies elsewhere: this body that is ageing so fast is the same one, for sure. Jack fulfils Coppola's dearest wish: to travel across time without losing one's integrity.

Jack (1996).

Matt Damon in *John Grisham's The Rainmaker* (1997).

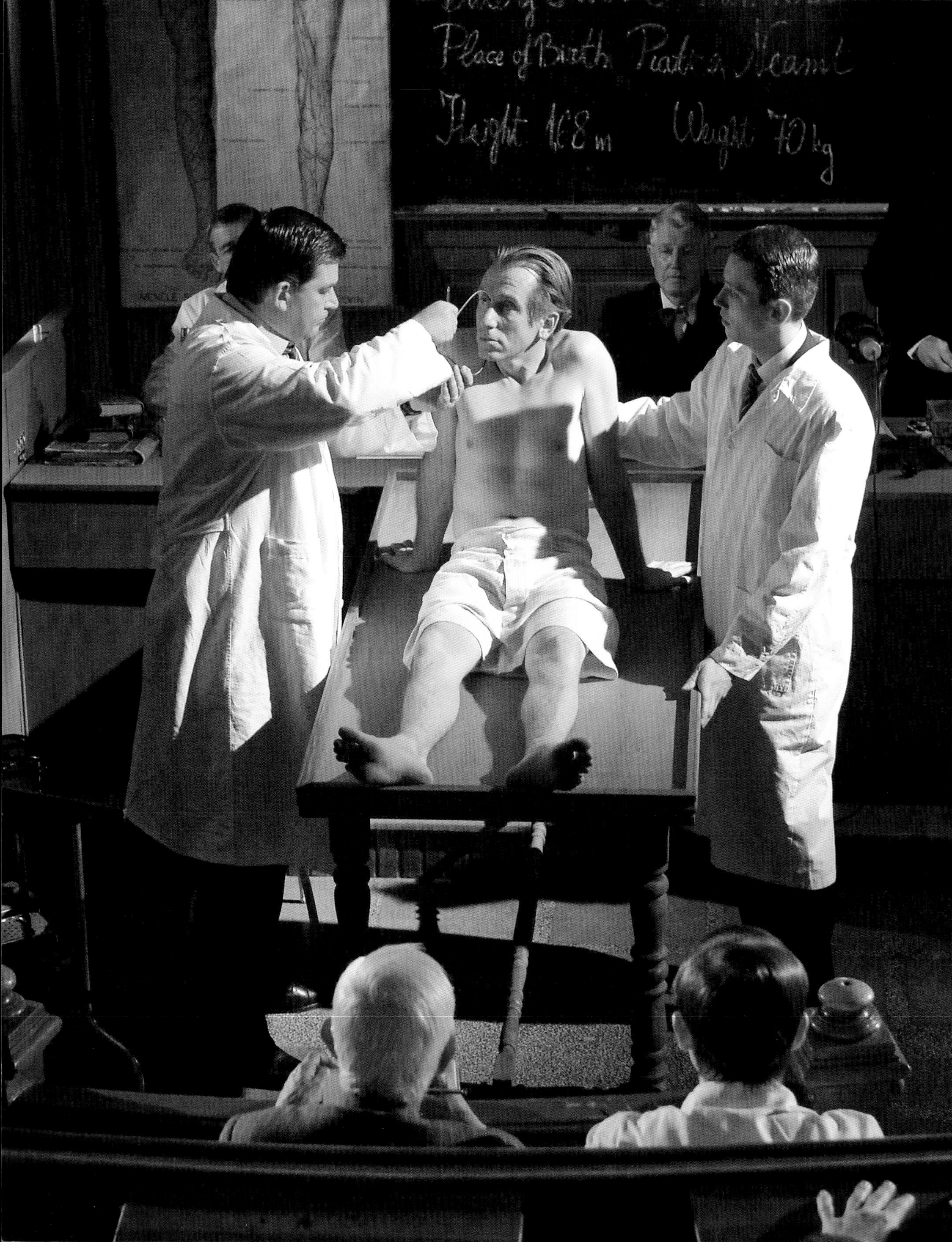
Place of Birth
Height 1.68 m
Weight 70 kg

Rejuvenation

From *Youth Without Youth* to *Tetro*

In 2005, Coppola had become fatally bogged down in his great *Megalopolis* project when he came across a novella by Mircea Eliade that held up a mirror to his own lack of direction. It was the story of Dominic Matei, a brilliant scholar who, at the age of seventy, is unable to complete his book on the origins of language, his only book and his life's work. Coppola started, in secret, to prepare the adaptation, which he intended to be the opposite of *Megalopolis*: it was to have a small budget, would be shot far away from Hollywood, in Romania, and the technical crew, apart from the loyal Walter Murch, would be Romanian. *Youth Without Youth* is a new departure.

The case of Professor Matei is certainly an unusual one. Struck by lightning, as if God had laid his finger on him, he nevertheless comes out of hospital unscathed and half-rejuvenated — and thus regenerated he returns to complete his great work. The way in which Coppola recapitulates his own obsessions is dazzling. As played by the short-statured Tim Roth, this latter-day Prometheus, stealing fire from Mount Olympus and challenging the gods, has something of Michael Corleone about him, while also resembling Colonel Kurtz in his meditative withdrawal and his search for

his roots. His over-reaching ambition has devastating effects: the birth of an evil double, as if the lightning had simply cut him in two; his meeting with a young woman, a human guinea pig whom, with his pathological thirst for knowledge, he will cause to age prematurely.

Above all, like Jack, Matei is a time-traveller, and like Peggy Sue, he falls for the myth of the second chance. As a young man, he had abandoned his fiancée for his work: he now meets a woman, played by the same actress (Alexandra Maria Lara), who gives him the chance to redeem himself. Lastly, by shooting the film in Romania, Coppola finds again the romantic Transylvania of his *Dracula*, whose fantastic themes — vampirism, eternal love and the transmigration of souls — he explores in greater depth. Yet the scope of this work is broader: Veronica is not only the double of his first love, but, like Mina in *Dracula*, she is possessed by a wandering soul, travels through history, speaks Sanskrit, ancient Egyptian and Babylonian, and sets out to go back to the earliest articulated words. Time-travelling is now on the scale of humanity as a whole.

In a nicely phrased statement he made before shooting started, Coppola explained that it was as if

he had died at the age of fifty and been reborn, and, as a result, at sixty-six he was actually sixteen. Matei is Coppola himself: he had regained the spirit of a zealous student, throwing himself headlong into his work. Shooting outside the system, he rediscovered his love of cinema and of experimentation. Starting from a firm base (he imposed on himself the constraint of using a stationary camera), he revised his direction shot by shot, while retaining a consistent anti-naturalism that drew him towards a dreamlike expressionism. The story is hard to pigeonhole, leaping from the Romania of 1938 (where Matei flees from the Nazis, who are interested in this Faustian mutant) to Switzerland, India and Malta, and back to square one, Romania. This elliptical plot is punctuated by dreams and full of false trails: suggestions that this is a war film, a superhero film (the lightning gives Matei superhuman powers) or a fantasy film (the pact with the devil, the evil double) are not developed, as the narration parallels the hero's mental confusion.

Matei's life emerges in fragments from this heterogeneous whole, drifting between life and death as time is suspended. As so often, it is at dusk that Coppola is at his most powerful. With a disturbing echo of the veranda scene that ends *The Godfather Part II*, Matei finds himself on a balcony with his prematurely aged mistress, her hair now grey, both of them lit by a studio sunset that could come from *The Outsiders*. At the end of the film, he encounters all his old friends in the back room of the Café Select. We're reminded of Visconti's *Death in Venice* (1971), Leone's *Once Upon a Time in America* (1984) and Kubrick's *The Shining* (1980), all of them films in which the ageing hero shuts himself up in a mental space where he projects at will his phantoms and fantasies. While it leaned towards the secrets of the origins of language, this broken life well and truly came back to a private search for lost time.

Families

Liberated by writing *Youth Without Youth*, Coppola embarked simultaneously on an original screenplay, his first since *The Conversation*, which he called *Tetro* (2009). *Youth Without Youth* thus functioned as a rebirth, even if it was not a very successful one. It was a 'film of convalescence', enabling Coppola to prepare the ground for his real return.

In fact, *Tetro* marks a return to the family stories that ensured the greatness of the *Godfather* trilogy and of *Rumble Fish*. Bennie (played by newcomer Alden Ehrenreich) is under the spell of his elder brother, Tetro, and turns up in Buenos Aires, where Tetro is living. Tetro was to have been played by Matt Dillon, suggesting that the cool Rusty James of *Rumble Fish* might have turned into a disillusioned Motorcycle Boy. In the end the role was played by the magisterial Vincent Gallo. But this story of brothers is accompanied by one about the settling of accounts with their father, a famous orchestral conductor, who has always mocked Tetro's wish to become a writer.

The great success of *Tetro* lies in the way it shares the director's characteristic themes while at the same time taking an uneven, unpredictable form. At its start, it suggests a piece of chamber theatre, with the two brothers meeting in a Buenos Aires set in no obvious period. Then, as the film continues, it swells, expands and gushes out in a torrent. That recomposed 'cell' is no more than the prelude to the decomposition of a family that is falling apart. Information comes in a disorderly fashion: their mother has died in a tragic car accident to which Tetro was a witness, his girlfriend has been stolen from him by his father and is also in a terminal coma. Violence wells up everywhere, and flashbacks, dreams and theatrical performances are planted throughout the story like explosives, as if shouting out a secret that we cannot hear. This colossal family secret will be revealed in the final scenes, when the father's death makes it possible for it to be told.

But in order to arrive at that point, the film, which Coppola chose to make in black and white, has had to contain sequences that destabilize space in an entirely unrealistic way, and to include music that gives it an increasingly operatic breadth. Bennie finishes the book that Tetro was writing (we find the same mythology of the Book as in *Youth Without Youth*) and the two brothers go off to perform their play in Patagonia. Their journey to the far south is accompanied by flashes of blinding light from the icebergs and by crystalline music sung by a children's choir. Following this return to roots, a last act comparable with the final passage of *The Godfather Part III*, brings the family's story to an end. At his father's public funeral, heightened by orchestral music, Tetro, still wearing the leather jacket in which he is first seen, climbs onto the stage where his father's coffin is displayed, and takes from him the baton he holds in his hands.

Francis Ford Coppola with Maribel Verdu and Alden Ehrenreich on the set of *Tetro* (2009).

Opposite page: Alden Ehrenreich in *Tetro* (2009).

A film by Coppola always has *one* theme, and *one* visual idea, and *Tetro* is no exception to the rule. In this case, the former is 'competiveness' and the latter, 'light'.[39] Competitiveness between brothers is at its core: that between Tetro and his little brother, who finishes his masterpiece for him, and that between the conductor-father and his brother (both played by Klaus Maria Brandauer). Coppola was inspired by his own passionate admiration for his elder brother, and by the competition between his father, Carmine Coppola, an orchestral conductor, and his uncle. And the visual idea, light, refers to the blinding headlights in the scene of Tetro's mother's accident and to the moths attracted by the light, beating their wings against the glass, a direct metaphor for the two brothers, who burn their wings as they circle round the family secret.

It is touching that this film erodes the figure of the father, in the opposite way to the *Godfather* trilogy. This time the father is the one who castrates, and the son sets fire to his portrait. Coppola does not pose as a patriarch but places himself firmly on the side of youth and rebellion. The wild Tetro roams around brandishing an axe, an image reminiscent of one of his earliest films, *Dementia 13*: the rejection of conformity is the same.

In contrast to *Youth Without Youth*, Coppola made a media event of his 'return'. Excluded from competition at Cannes in 2009, and bearing in mind the example of Tetro, who turned down the honours of the Patagonia Festival, he agreed that his film should open the Directors' Fortnight. It was there, among young directors, that he wanted his film to be seen, because he was once again a 'young director'. His devotion to Cannes and to Paris when the film was released meant that it enjoyed great success in France. It also received good reviews in the United States, even though the ratings were obviously lower than those of his past Hollywood productions. Coppola had achieved what he had been trying to do from the beginning, to be a director free of attachments, directing and producing personal stories of which he was the sole creator. It was quite a journey to get there.

90   Maribel Verdu and Vincent Gallo in *Tetro* (2009).

What makes a Coppola film?

1. First, there's the subject. As Coppola himself says in his commentary to the DVD of *Finian's Rainbow*: 'Films are like haiku; they express a thought or an emotion in very few words.'

2. Then there is the 'destination'. That's a better word than 'commission'. For whom was the film made? When it's for oneself, and therefore for nobody, failures are all the more serious. To make a film for oneself may be the whim of a megalomaniac (*One from the Heart*) or a challenge (*The Cotton Club*). In both cases, it is the director as experimenter who is most delighted by his experimentation.

His other films usually have a 'destination', the person or persons for whom they are intended: his father (*Finian's Rainbow*), his mother (*The Rain People*), his children (*The Outsiders*), his brother (*Rumble Fish*), his dead son (*Gardens of Stone, Tucker*), his daughter (*Life Without Zoe*), his granddaughter (*Jack*), or his family as a whole (*The Godfather*).

The idea of making a film for somebody isn't very common. We must take seriously the dedication of *The Outsiders* to his young readers and the restoration of the long version to please them, on the DVD *The Outsiders*: *The Complete Novel*. The same goes for the work done on behalf of the Tucker family, or the U.S. Army in *Gardens of Stone*. There's no question of betrayal; Coppola is not trying to outsmart anybody. Nor does he fulfil his contract and no more; he offers the film as a gift.

3. And then there's his style. The style is to be chosen according to the subject, not the other way round, as with Scorsese, for whom style comes first, whether the subject is Edith Wharton's New York (*The Age of Innocence*) or the life of Howard Hughes (*Aviator*). It is also to be chosen according to the destination, since, unlike Scorsese, with his 'pirate' model, Coppola feels a director should not disguise himself. Coppola has been widely criticized for his changeability, and it is undeniable that one cannot recognize his style from a few shots, unlike Scorsese or De Palma. His idea of style is that it is malleable, it is not what makes the artist. In this sense, Coppola is a dinosaur. He belongs to a time before the romantic obsession with style and the assertion of the artist's subjective will. The romantic bends the subject to his style, and creates for himself. Coppola adapts his style to his subject and creates for someone else. The style is to be chosen from among the secrets of cinema history, from the palette of styles offered by 100 years of film-making.[36]

4. Finally, there is technique. Style is no longer the prerogative of an individual subjectivity: it has become the outcome of technique. Cinematic technique is collective, and it has two levels: the close associates, and the technicians hired for the occasion, who give each project its particular tone.[37] Coppola sees himself as the conductor of an orchestra.

5. And there is sometimes an image. The image is the result of the delicate balance between the subject, the style and the technique. The 'image' of *Tucker* is the car itself; *The Outsiders* is 'a film about the sunset', as much an indication of a quality of light as it is of melancholy; *One from the Heart* is 'a film about neon signs', signs that have as much to do with brightness as with superficiality.

The subject is always what is most important. Is there a common subject? We might say it is the rise and fall of mortals who take themselves for gods, dreamers who try to force their dreams to come true. That's the motto of *Finian's Rainbow*: 'Follow the fellow who follows the dream', because to follow one's dream is not something given to everyone. But that isn't it. The common element is time. *The Godfather*, *The Outsiders* and *Peggy Sue* represent the furthest points in the search for lost time. Coppola's entire oeuvre is divided between vitality, speed, life and youth (which is of major importance to him) and decline, melancholy and death. It is as if life were reduced to these two ages. At over thirty, Tucker and Peggy Sue behave like adolescents; below that age, Michael Corleone and Motorcycle Boy are bowed down by the weight of their years.

And the two ages are linked by the element of transmission. Willard and Kurtz, Michael and Vito, Vincent and Michael, Hazard and Willow – it is less a case of succession (from a perspective of power) than of transmission. When the father is absent, it is left to the dying adolescent to whisper in the ear of one of his peers, as in *The Outsiders*.

We can understand how each film is a moral fable: transmission has to be transmitted. Coppola sees himself as a father and a Godfather; we learn not only that war is confused and power drives people mad, but that transmission links us all together. It is a 'filial' moral, but it goes beyond the family to include friendship, social solidarity and history. The idea of a film's 'destination' has to do with transmission; that of style also, since we inherit a formal legacy from the past. Transmission is what enables us to combat time.

Francis Ford Coppola wrote these lines in his diary, on 18 September 1991, while he was preparing to make *Bram Stoker's Dracula*:

ONE CAN BE FROZEN IN TIME.
ONE CAN BE BEYOND TIME.
ONE CAN BE AHEAD OF TIME.
ONE CAN BE BEHIND TIME.
BUT, ONE CANNOT BE
WITHOUT TIME.
[...]
TIME WAITS FOR NO MAN.[38]

Francis Ford Coppola on the set of
Tucker: The Man and His Dream (1988).

Chronology

1939
7 April. Born in Detroit, Michigan, the third son of Carmine Coppola, a flautist and conductor, and Italia Coppola, who had been an actress in Italy.

1949
Contracts polio and spends a year in bed. Begins to make amateur collage films in 8mm.

1957
Begins theatre studies at Hofstra University, where he meets several future collaborators, including the actor James Caan. His production of *A Streetcar Named Desire* attracts favourable attention. He sets up a film club, and has said that on Mondays he would make theatre, and on Tuesdays he wished he was making films. Seeing Eisenstein's *October* helps him decide.

1960
Enrols in the film school at UCLA (University of California of Los Angeles), which was still in its infancy, where he is not happy with the teaching. Makes a short film in homage to Eisenstein, *Aymonn the Terrible*, about a narcissistic sculptor who casts a three-metre-high statue of himself. A hint of megalomania to come?

1961–1962
Urged to do more serious things, he works for the seedy 'nudie' industry and puts his name to two hybrid films: *Tonight for Sure* and *The Bellboy and the Playgirls*.

1962
Meets Roger Corman and becomes his assistant, before making his first real feature film, *Dementia 13*, in the space of nine days.

1963
2 February. Marries Eleanor Neil, a UCLA graduate whom he had met while making *Dementia 13*. **17 September.** Birth of Gian-Carlo, nicknamed Gio. Coppola starts work as a screenwriter for Seven Arts with *Reflections in a Golden Eye*, made by John Huston in 1967.

1965
22 April. Birth of his second son, Roman.

1966
Makes *You're a Big Boy Now*, produced by Seven Arts.

1968
Makes *Finian's Rainbow*, produced by Warner-Seven Arts, now one company. It is Fred Astaire's last musical and the worst, in his opinion.

1969
Shoots *The Rain People* in various places. **14 November.** Sets up American Zoetrope in San Francisco. Coppola is its president, George Lucas its vice-president. Since 1972, its headquarters have been in the Sentinel Building.

1970
19 November. The day Coppola calls 'Black Thursday'. A year to the day after Zoetrope was founded, Warner-Seven Arts withdraws after seeing its first production, George Lucas's *THX 1138*. Zoetrope goes bankrupt and has to repay $600,000.

1971
Coppla wins his first Oscar for the screenplay of *Patton*. 14 May. Birth of his daughter, Sofia.

1972
The Godfather is an unprecedented surprise success and wins the Oscar for best film. Its young director becomes a 'godfather' to the new generation and his position in the industry is secure.

1973
Great popular success of *American Graffiti*, directed by George Lucas and produced by Coppola.

1974
Two big successes: *The Conversation* takes the Palme d'Or at the Cannes Festival; *The Godfather Part II* is less successful with the public than *The Godfather* but more so with the critics. It wins six Oscars, including best film and best director.

1975
Coppola buys a vineyard in Napa Valley, California. He creates the appellation Niebaum-Coppola, now Rubicon.

1976
1 March. He takes his family to the Philippines to start shooting *Apocalypse Now*. He thinks it will take a few weeks.

1977
21 May. Last day's shooting on *Apocalypse Now*. Coppola comes back to San Francisco with 'a million feet of film' or two hundred and fifty hours' worth.

Francis Ford Coppola at the 1967 Cannes Film Festival.

Francis Ford Coppola on the set of *The Rain People* (1969).

Francis Ford Coppola in front of the Zoetrope Studio van 'The Silverfish' in the early 1980s.

Francis Ford Coppola with his wife Eleanor at the 1975 Academy Awards.

Francis Ford Coppola on the set of *Apocalypse Now* (1979).

1979

13 May. World premiere of *Apocalypse Now* at Cannes. Coppola wins the Palme d'Or for the second time. At the Oscars in April, he announces that electronic cinema has arrived.

1980

25 March. He buys Hollywood General studios in Los Angeles and turns it into 'Zoetrope Studios'. For the first time, he has a base in Hollywood. He starts work on *One from the Heart*, 'manufactured' entirely in his studios.

1982

14 January. Coppola organizes the premiere of *One from the Heart* at New York's Radio City Music Hall; it is shown twice, to an audience of six thousand. It's a flop. **20 April.** Coppola announces the liquidation of Zoetrope Studios. He has already moved his headquarters to Tulsa, Oklahoma, where he starts shooting *The Outsiders* on 19 March. While he is shooting it, he writes the screenplay of *Rumble Fish* with S. E. Hinton. **12 June.** Shooting of *Rumble Fish* starts immediately.

1983–1984

The difficult gestation of *The Cotton Club*. After a shoot lasting four months, the film is completed at the last minute on Christmas Eve, 1983. A long cut, pieced together from several versions, is released a year later, in December 1984.

1985

A nice quick job: *Peggy Sue Got Married*.

1986

26 May. Death of his elder son, Gio, in a speedboat accident during the shoot of *Gardens of Stone*. His daughter-in-law was pregnant at the time with a daughter, Gia, to whom *Jack* was later dedicated.

1987

Coppola writes and films *Tucker: A Man and His Dream*, marking his reunion with his friend George Lucas, its producer.

1989–1990

The Godfather Part III. Coppola spends a year preparing the film and writing the screenplay with Mario Puzo. **27 November.** Shooting starts at the Cinecittà studios in Rome. Like the previous Godfather films, it is released at Christmas, in 1990. Coppola is hurt by the sharp criticism of Sofia's performance as Michael Corleone's daughter.

1992

13 November. Release of *Bram Stoker's Dracula*. Six days later, while at his holiday home in Guatemala, Coppola learns that box-office receipts reached $31.5 million in a single weekend. He notes in his diary: 'It was a success and it saved my skin.' It marks the end of ten years of debt.

1996–1997

Coppola is bankable again, with *Jack* ($60 million in the United States) and *John Grisham's The Rainmaker* ($46 million). He consolidates his position in Hollywood, and begins a science-fiction project to match his ambitions: *Megalopolis*.

1998

Warner revokes its contract with Zoetrope for the production of a Pinocchio film, to be made by Coppola. The studio is required to pay Coppola $80 million. This is Zoetrope's revenge on Warner for the debacle of 1970, and Coppola's revenge on the system, as triumphant as the outcome of the trial in *John Grisham's The Rainmaker*.

2001

A new cut of *Apocalypse Now – Apocalypse Now Redux* – is presented at Cannes and released in cinemas.

2007

Started in 2005 and shot entirely in Romania, *Youth Without Youth* is presented at the Rome Film Festival.

2009

Tetro opens the Directors' Fortnight at Cannes.

Francis Ford Coppola with Matt Damon and Danny De Vito on the set of *John Grisham's The Rainmaker* (1997).

Francis Ford Coppola with his son Gio at the 1979 Cannes Film Festival.

Francis Ford Coppola on the set of *One from the Heart* (1982).

Francis Ford Coppola on the set of *Bram Stoker's Dracula* (1992).

Francis Ford Coppola with Wim Wenders on the set of Wim Wenders' *Hammett* (1982).

Francis Ford Coppola with Sofia Coppola and his sister Talia Shire on the set of *The Godfather Part III* (1990).

Filmography

SHORT FILMS

Captain Eo 1986
Format 35mm. **Running time** 17 mins. With Michael Jackson and Anjelica Huston.
• Captain Eo and the crew of his space-ship visit the Witch Queen.

Life Without Zoe 1989
Screenplay Francis Ford Coppola, Sofia Coppola. **Format** 35mm. **Running time** 34 mins. With Heather McComb and Talia Shire.
• A little rich girl wanders round New York and tries to bring her parents back together. A segment of *New York Stories*, with Martin Scorsese's *Life Lessons* and Woody Allen's *Oedipus Wrecks*.

TELEVISION FILMS

'Rip Van Winkle' 1985
Running time 48 mins. With Harry Dean Stanton and Talia Shire.
• After taking a little nap, Rip Van Winkle wakes up twenty years later. His wife has died, and he finds his son has grown up. An episode in the TV series *Faerie Tale Theatre* (HBO), broadcast in 1987.

The Godfather: A Novel for Television 1977
Running time 6h 14. With Marlon Brando, Al Pacino, Robert Duvall, James Caan, Diane Keaton, Robert De Niro, Talia Shire.
• This series combines *The Godfather* and *The Godfather Part II* with additional footage added into one film.

FEATURE FILMS

Tonight for Sure 1961
Screenplay Jerry Shaffer, Francis Ford Coppola. **Cinematography** Jack Hill. **Editing** Ronald Waller. **Music** Carmine Coppola. **Production** Francis Ford Coppola. **Running time** 1h 15. With Jack Schanzer (Benjamin Jabowski), Donald Kenney (Samuel Hill), Electra, Exotica, Laura Cornell, Karla Lee.
• Two boys who have become born-again Christians meet at a strip-tease club to protest against vice. Each of them tells how he has come to be there. A collage of Coppola's short *The Peeper* with an erotic Western, *The Wide Open Spaces*. The completed film contains additional scenes shot by Coppola.

The Bellboy and the Playgirls 1962
Screenplay Francis Ford Coppola, Fritz Umgelter. **Cinematography** Jack Hill. **Production** Wolfgang Hartwig. **Running time** 1h 34. With Willy Fritsch (Gregor), Karen Dor (Dinah), Don Kenney (George), June Wilkinson (Mme Whimplepoole).
• While a theatre director is trying to persuade his leading lady to play a risqué scene, George, the bellboy at the hotel next door, is watching from the wings and sets about making himself popular with the girls. The first segment, in black and white, is an extract from Fritz Umgelter's *Mit Eva fing die Sünde* (*Sin Began with Eve*, 1958); the second, in colour, was shot by Coppola.

Battle Beyond The Sun 1963
Direction Mikhail Karzhukov, Aleksandr Kozyr, Thomas Colchart (Francis Ford Coppola). **Screenplay** Mikhail Karzhukov, Yevgeni Pomeshchikov, Aleksei Sazanov. **Screenplay and editing** (American version) Francis Ford Coppola. **Cinematography** Nikolai Kulchitsky.

Production Mosfilm, Roger Corman (American version). **Running time** 1h 17. With Ivan Pereverzev (Kornev; Dr Andrew Gordon in the American version), Aleksandr Shvorin (Gordienko; Craig Matthews in the American version).
• The Earth's two hemispheres are competing against each other in space. When they reach Mars, the astronauts are faced with two monsters, who are, to say the least, unexpected. A rewritten and re-edited version of the Soviet film *Nebo zovyot*, with additional scenes shot by Coppola.

Dementia 13 1963
Screenplay Francis Ford Coppola. **Cinematography** Charles Hannawalt. **Editing** Mort Tubor, Stuart O'Brien. **Music** Ronald Stein. **Production** Francis Ford Coppola for Roger Corman. **Running time** 1h 15. With William Campbell (Richard Haloran), Luana Anders (Louise Haloran), Bart Patton (Billy Haloran), Mary Mitchell (Kane), Patrick Magee (Justin Caleb).
• Louise has her eyes on an inheritance from her mother-in-law. In a castle in Ireland, she finds an inbred family, disturbed by the death of a child.

You're a Big Boy Now 1966
Screenplay Francis Ford Coppola, from the novel by David Benedictus. **Cinematography** Andy Laszlo. **Production design** Vassele Fotopoulos. **Costumes** Theoni V. Aldredge. **Editing** Aram Avakian. **Production** Phil Feldman for Seven Arts. **Running time** 1h 36. With Peter Kastner (Bernard Chanticleer), Elizabeth Hartman (Barbara Darling), Geraldine Page (Margery Chanticleer), Julie Harris (Miss Thing), Rip Torn (I. H. Chanticleer), Karen Black (Amy).
• The adventures of a man obsessed with a young blonde he has met at college: New York night-life, his complicated relationship with the beauty, and the parental pressure from which the big boy has to escape.

Finian's Rainbow 1968
Screenplay E.Y. Harburg, Fred Saidy, from their musical. **Cinematography** Philip Lathrop. **Production design** Hilyard M. Brown. **Costumes** Dorothy Jenkins. **Editing** Melvin Shapiro. **Music** Burton Lane. **Production** Joseph Landon for Warner-Seven Arts. **Running time** 2h 25. With Fred Astaire (Finian McLonergan), Petula Clark (Sharon McLonergan), Tommy Steele (Og), Don Francks (Woody Mahoney), Barbara Hancock (Susan).
• A father and his daughter steal the fairies' gold in Ireland and bury it near Fort Knox to make it multiply. They settle in Rainbow Valley, where blacks and whites live in equality.

The Rain People 1969
Screenplay Francis Ford Coppola. **Cinematography** Wilmer Butler. **Production design** Leon Ericksen. **Editing** Blackie Malkin. **Sound editing** Walter Murch. **Music** Ronald Stein. **Production** Bart Patton and Ronald Colby for American Zoetrope, Warner-Seven Arts. **Running time** 1h 41. With Shirley Knight (Natalie Ravenna), James Caan ('Killer' Kilgannon), Robert Duvall (Gordon), Marya Zimmet (Rosalie), Tom Aldredge (Mr Alfred).
• A pregnant woman leaves the marital home and on the road picks up a not-very-bright former footballer. She's stuck with him, takes care of him, and tries to get rid of him.

The Godfather 1972
Screenplay Mario Puzo, Francis Ford Coppola, from the novel by Mario Puzo. **Cinematography** Gordon Willis. **Sound** Christopher Newman. **Production design** Dean Tavoularis. **Costumes** Anna Hill Johnstone. **Editing** William Reynolds, Peter Zinner. **Music** Nino Rota, Carmine Coppola. **Post-production consultant** Walter Murch. **Production** Albert S. Ruddy for

Paramount. **Running time** 2h 55. With Marlon Brando (Don Vito Corleone), Al Pacino (Michael Corleone), James Caan (Sonny Corleone), Richard Castellano (Clemenza), Robert Duvall (Tom Hagen), Sterling Hayden (McCluskey), John Marley (Jack Wotz), Richard Conte (Barzini), Al Lettieri (Sollozzo), Diane Keaton (Kay Adams), Abe Vigoda (Tessio), Talia Shire (Connie), John Cazale (Fredo Corleone), Gianni Russo (Carlo Rizzi).

• Don Vito Corleone is a respected Godfather. But when he refuses to get involved in drug dealing, New York's Five Families unite against him. Weakened and hurt, he passes the baton to his youngest son, Michael, who goes on the offensive. When his father dies, he becomes the new Godfather.

The Conversation   1974
Screenplay Francis Ford Coppola. **Cinematography** Bill Butler. **Production design** Dean Tavoularis. **Costumes** Aggie Guerard Rodgers. **Editing and mixing** Walter Murch. **Music** David Shire. **Production** Francis Ford Coppola and Fred Roos for Zoetrope, Paramount. **Running time** 1h 53. With Gene Hackman (Harry Caul), John Cazale (Stan), Allen Garfield (Bernie Moran), Frederic Forrest (Mark), Cindy Williams (Ann), Harrison Ford (Martin Stett), Robert Duvall (The director).

• The head of a large company hires Harry Caul to carry out surveillance on his wife and her lover. His recordings show that the couple feel they are under threat from the husband. Gnawed at by his failure on a previous case, Caul is unable to prevent the murder taking place. But he had got the conspiracy wrong: it was the couple who wanted to get rid of the husband.

The Godfather Part II   1974
Screenplay Mario Puzo, Francis Ford Coppola, from the novel by Mario Puzo. **Cinematography** Gordon Willis. **Production design** Dean Tavoularis. **Costumes** Theadora Van Runkle. **Editing** Peter Zinner, Barry Malkin, Richard Marks. **Sound editing** Walter Murch. **Music** Nino Rota, Carmine Coppola. **Production** Francis Ford Coppola for American Zoetrope, Paramount. **Running time** 3h 20. With Al Pacino (Michael Corleone), Robert De Niro (Vito Corleone), Robert Duvall (Tom Hagen), Diane Keaton (Kay Adams), John Cazale (Fredo Corleone), Talia Shire (Connie), Lee Strasberg (Hyman Roth), Michael V. Gazzo (Frank Pentangeli).

• The youth of Vito Corleone in 1920s New York is shown in parallel with Michael's growing appetite for power and his paranoia. Now living in Nevada with his family, he plans to extend his influence to Las Vegas and Cuba. Against the background of the Cuban revolution, he learns that his brother Fredo has betrayed him.

Apocalypse Now   1979
Screenplay John Milius, Francis Ford Coppola, after *Heart of Darkness* by Joseph Conrad. **Narration** Michael Herr. **Cinematography** Vittorio Storaro. **Sound** Walter Murch. **Production design** Dean Tavoularis. Angelo Graham. **Costumes** Charles E. James. **Editing** Richard Marks, Walter Murch, Gerald B. Greenberg, Lisa Fruchtman, Barry Malkin. **Editing, long version** Walter Murch. **Sound editing, long version** Michael Kirchberger. **Music** Carmine Coppola, Francis Ford Coppola. **Production** Francis Ford Coppola for Zoetrope, United Artists. **Production, long version** Kim Aubry for American Zoetrope, Miramax. **Running time** 2h 33 (3h 12, long version). With Martin Sheen (Captain Willard), Marlon Brando (Colonel Kurtz), Robert Duvall (Lieutenant-colonel Kilgore), Frederic Forrest ('Chef' Hicks), Albert Hall (Chief Phillips), Sam Bottoms (Lance), Larry Fishburne ('Clean'), Dennis Hopper (The photojournalist), Harrison Ford (Colonel Lucas) and Christian Marquand and Aurore Clement in the long version.

• During the Vietnam War, Captain Willard is given the task of getting rid of Colonel Kurtz, who has gone out of control. The journey up-river to Cambodia, where Kurtz has built his hide-out, provides many surprises. In 2001, a long version of the film, *Apocalypse Now Redux*, was released.

One from the Heart   1982
Screenplay Armyan Bernstein, Francis Ford Coppola. **Cinematography** Vittorio Storaro. **Sound** Richard Beggs. **Production design** Dean Tavoularis. **Costumes** Ruth Morley. **Editing** Anne Goursaud. **Music** Tom Waits. **Production** Gray Frederickson and Fred Roos for Zoetrope, Columbia. **Running time** 1h 41. With Frederic Forrest (Hank), Teri Garr (Frannie), Raul Julia (Ray), Nastassja Kinski (Leila), Lainie Kazan (Maggie), Harry Dean Stanton (Moe).

• Hank and Frannie decide to separate. Under the bright lights of Las Vegas, he meets an attractive trapeze artist, and she meets a charming waiter. The brief appeal of the faraway eventually leads to a reconciliation.

The Outsiders   1983
Screenplay Kathleen Knutsen Roswell, from the novel by S. E. Hinton. **Cinematography** Stephen H. Burum. **Production design** Dean Tavoularis. **Costumes** Marge Bowers. **Editing** Anne Goursaud. **Additional editing, long version** Bob Bonz, Melissa Kent. **Music** Carmine Coppola. **Music, long version** Richard Beggs. **Production** Fred Roos and Gray Frederickson for Zoetrope, Warner Bros. **Production, long version** Francis Ford Coppola and Kim Aubry for Zoetrope. **Running time** 1h 31 (1h 53, long version). With C. Thomas Howell (Ponyboy Curtis), Matt Dillon (Dallas Winston), Ralph Macchio (Johnny Cade), Patrick Swayze (Darrel Curtis), Rob Lowe (Sodapop Curtis), Emilio Estevez (Two-Bit Matthews), Tom Cruise (Steve Randle), Diane Lane (Cherry Valance), Leif Garrett (Bob Sheldon).

• The Greasers are a rival gang to the Socs, kids from rich families. When Ponyboy and Johnny kill one of the Socs, they have to lie low in the countryside, but fate catches up with them. A long version, entitled *The Outsiders: The Complete Novel*, was released on DVD only in 2005, restoring the director's cut and replacing Carmine Coppola's music by rock classics from the 1960s.

Rumble Fish   1983
Screenplay S. E. Hinton, Francis Ford Coppola, from the novel by S. E. Hinton. **Cinematography** Stephen H. Burum. **Sound** David Parker, Richard Beggs. **Production design** Dean Tavoularis. **Costumes** Marge Bowers. **Editing** Barry Malkin. **Music** Stewart Copeland. **Production** Fred Roos and Doug Claybourne for Zoetrope, Universal. **Running time** 1h 34. With Matt Dillon (Rusty James), Mickey Rourke (Motorcycle Boy), Diane Lane (Patty), Dennis Hopper (The father), Diana Scarwid (Cassandra), Vincent Spano (Steve), Nicolas Cage (Smokey), Christopher Penn (B. J. Jackson), Larry Fishburne (Midget), Tom Waits (Benny).

• Rusty James hero-worships his brother, Motorcycle Boy, the former king of the neighbourhood. He comes back from California disillusioned and teaches Rusty that it's no good being a gang leader and he should clear out.

The Cotton Club   1984
Screenplay William Kennedy, Francis Coppola, Mario Puzo. **Cinematography** Stephen Goldblatt. **Sound** Edward Beyer. **Production design** Richard Sylbert. **Costumes** Milena Canonero. **Editing** Barry Malkin, Robert Q. Lovett. **Music** John Barry, Bob Wilber. **Production** Robert Evans for Zoetrope, Orion. **Running time** 2h 09. With Richard Gere (Dixie Dwyer), Gregory Hines (Sandman Williams), Diane Lane (Vera Cicero), Lonette McKee (Lila Rose Oliver), Bob Hoskins (Owney Madden), James Remar (Dutch Schultz), Nicolas Cage (Vincent Dwyer).

• It's 1928 in Harlem, at the Cotton Club, with its background of tap-dancing and gunshots. Dixie, a trumpet-player, is hired by a mobster to keep an eye on his mistress. He falls in love with her.

Peggy Sue Got Married — 1986

Screenplay Jerry Leichtling, Arlene Sarner. **Cinematography** Jordan Cronenweth. **Sound** Michael Kirchberger. **Production design** Dean Tavoularis. **Costumes** Theodora Van Runkle. **Editing** Barry Malkin. **Music** John Barry. **Production** Paul R. Gurian for Zoetrope, Tri-Star. **Running time** 1h 44. With Kathleen Turner (Peggy Sue Kelcher), Nicolas Cage (Charlie Bodell), Barry Miller (Richard Norvik), Catherine Hicks (Carol Heath), Joan Allen (Maddie Nagle), Kevin J. O'Connor (Michael Fitzsimmons), Jim Carrey (Walter Getz), Barbara Harris (Evelyn Kelcher), Don Murray (Jack Kelcher), Maureen O'Sullivan (Elizabeth Alvorg), Sofia Coppola (Nancy Kelcher).

• Peggy Sue is about to get a divorce from Charlie, whom she met while they were in high school. At an anniversary dance, she finds herself magically transported back into the past. Determined not to make the same mistake twice, she rejects the childish Charlie. But when you're married, it's for life.

Gardens of Stone — 1987

Screenplay Ronald Bass, from the novel by Nicholas Proffitt. **Cinematography** Jordan Cronenweth. **Sound** Richard Beggs. **Production design** Dean Tavoularis. **Costumes** Willa Kim, Judianna Makovsky. **Editing** Barry Malkin. **Music** Carmine Coppola. **Production** Michael I. Levy and Francis Coppola for Tri-Star. **Running time** 1h 51. With James Caan (Clell Hazard), Anjelica Huston (Samantha Davis), James Earl Jones (Goody Nelson), D. B. Sweeney (Jackie Willow), Dean Stockwell (Homer Thomas), Mary Stuart Masterson (Rachel Feld), Sam Bottoms (Lieutenant Webber).

• Sergeant Hazard, a veteran of the Vietnam War, is now part of the honour guard at Arlington National Cemetery. His life is turned upside down by the arrival of a young recruit who wants to go to fight in Vietnam.

Tucker: The Man and His Dream — 1988

Screenplay Arnold Schulman, David Seidler. **Cinematography** Vittorio Storaro. **Sound** Richard Beggs. **Production design** Dean Tavoularis. **Costumes** Milena Canonero. **Editing** Priscilla Nedd. **Music** Joe Jackson. **Production** Fred Roos and Fred Fuchs for Lucasfilm, Zoetrope, Paramount. **Running time** 1h 51. With Jeff Bridges (Preston Tucker), Joan Allen (Vera), Martin Landau (Abe Karatz), Frederic Forrest (Eddie), Mako (Jimmy), Elias Koteas (Alex), Christian Slater (Junior), Lloyd Bridges (Senator Fergusson), Dean Stockwell (Howard Hugues).

• Tucker has a single dream: to produce his 'Torpedo' touring car. He embarks on the project with no funds, with help from friends and family. But the big Detroit manufacturers see the brilliant inventor as a threat, and obstruct him. Only fifteen Torpedoes see the light of day.

The Godfather Part III — 1990

Screenplay Mario Puzo, Francis Ford Coppola. **Cinematography** Gordon Willis. **Sound** Richard Beggs. **Production design** Dean Tavoularis. **Costumes** Milena Canonero. **Editing** Barry Malkin, Lisa Fruchtman, Walter Murch. **Music** Carmine Coppola. **Production** Francis Ford Coppola for Zoetrope, Paramount. **Running time** 2h 41. With Al Pacino (Michael Corleone), Diane Keaton (Kay Adams), Talia Shire (Connie Corleone), Andy Garcia (Vincent Mancini), Sofia Coppola (Mary Corleone), Eli Wallach (Don Altobello), Joe Mantegna (Joey Zasa), Bridget Fonda (Grace Hamilton), Raf Vallone (Cardinal Lamberto), John Savage (Andrew Hagen).

• It's 1979. Since the death of his brother Fredo, Michael Corleone has been looking for redemption. He goes into business with the Vatican as a way of putting an end to his illegal activities. The other New York Families don't see it that way. He finds

support in his wild nephew, Vincent, who has inconveniently fallen in love with his daughter Mary.

Bram Stoker's Dracula — 1992

Screenplay James V. Hart, from Bram Stoker's *Dracula*. **Cinematography** Michael Ballhaus. **Sound** David Stone. **Production design** Garrett Lewis. **Costumes** Eiko Ishioka. **Visual effects** Roman Coppola. **Editing** Nicholas C. Smith, Glenn Scantlebury, Anne Goursaud. **Music** Wojciech Kilar. **Production** Francis Ford Coppola, Fred Fuchs, Charles Mulvehill for Zoetrope, Columbia. **Running time** 2h 03. With Gary Oldman (Dracula), Winona Ryder (Mina, Elisabeta), Anthony Hopkins (Abraham Van Helsing), Keanu Reeves (Jonathan Harker), Sadie Frost (Lucy), Tom Waits (Renfield), Richard E. Grant (Jack Seward), Cary Elwes (Arthur Holmwood), Billy Campbell (Quincey Morris).

• A love story that travels across time. In 1492, the Count Dracula, aka Vlad the Impaler, loses Elisabeta, and is condemned to eternal life. The vampire finds her again in the guise of Mina, four hundred years later.

Jack — 1996

Screenplay James Demonaco, Gary Nadeau. **Cinematography** John Toll. **Production design** Dean Tavoularis. **Costumes** Aggie Guerard Rodgers. **Editing** Barry Malkin. **Production** Ricardo Mestres, Fred Fuchs, Francis Ford Coppola for Zoetrope, Buena Vista. **Running time** 1h 53. With Robin Williams (Jack Powell), Diane Lane (Karen Powell), Jennifer Lopez (Miss Marquez), Brian Kerwin (Brian Powell), Fran Dreschler (Dolores Durante), Bill Cosby (Lawrence Woodruff).

• Jack, aged ten, contracts a disease that makes him age four times as fast as normal. At first he is excluded by his peers, but he manages to integrate himself; to appear to be an adult has its advantages. But growing up four times as fast also means ageing at the same rate.

John Grisham's The Rainmaker — 1997

Screenplay Francis Ford Coppola, from the novel by John Grisham. **Narration** Michael Herr. **Cinematography** John Toll. **Production design** Howard Cummings. **Costumes** Aggie Guerard Rodgers. **Editing** Barry Malkin. **Music** Elmer Bernstein. **Production** Michael Douglas, Steven Reuther and Fred Fuchs for Zoetrope, Paramount. **Running time** 2h 10. With Matt Damon (Rudy Baylor), Claire Danes (Kelly Riker), Jon Voight (Leo F. Drummond), Mary Kay Place (Dot Black), Mickey Rourke (Bruiser Stone), Danny DeVito (Deck Schifflet), Dean Stockwell (Judge Harvey Hale), Teresa Wright (Miss Birdie), Danny Glover (Judge Tyrone Kipler).

• A young attorney takes on a powerful insurance company that refuses cover to a man with leukaemia. The man dies, but the lawyer's victory is so crushing that the company goes bankrupt and is unable to pay.

Youth Without Youth — 2007

Screenplay Francis Ford Coppola, from the novella by Mircea Eliade. **Cinematography** Mihai Malaimare Jr. **Sound** Mihai Bogos. **Production design** Calin Papura. **Costumes** Gloria Papura. **Editing** Walter Murch. **Music** Osvaldo Golijov. **Production** Francis Ford Coppola. **Running time** 2h 01. With Tim Roth (Dominic Matei), Alexandra Maria Lara (Veronica, Laura), Bruno Ganz (Professor Stanciulescu), Andre Hennicke (Josef Rudolf), Marcel Iures (Tucci), Alexandra Pirici (The woman in Room 6).

• In Bucharest, on the eve of World War II, Professor Dominic Matei is struck by lightning, just as he is contemplating suicide. Inexplicably, he comes out of hospital not only cured but rejuvenated. He had been over seventy, but now has the body of a twenty-five-year-old. He will be able to complete his great work, a book on the origins of language.

Tetro   **2009**
Screenplay Francis Ford Coppola.
Cinematography Mihai Malaimare
Jr. **Sound** Vincent d'Elia. **Production design** Sebelowtián Orgambide.
Costumes Cecilia Monti. **Editing**
Walter Murch. **Music** Osvaldo Golijov. **Production** American Zoetrope.
Running time 2h 07. With Vincent
Gallo (Tetro), Alden Ehrenreich (Bennie), Maribel Verdu (Miranda), Klaus
Maria Brandauer (Carlo), Carmen
Maura (Alone), Rodrigo De la Serna
(José), Leticia Brédice (Josefina).
• Bennie is reunited with his elder
brother, now living in exile in Buenos
Aires, where he has changed his
name to Tetro. Their reunion brings
to light everything Tetro was trying to
escape: his wish to become a writer,
the crushing influence of his father,
a famous orchestral conductor, his
mother's death, and the mysterious
family tragedy that was the reason
for his leaving.

PRODUCER ONLY

The Terror	**1963**
by Roger Corman	
The Making of	
'The Rain People'	**1969**
by George Lucas	
THX 1138	**1971**
by George Lucas	
American Graffiti	**1973**
by George Lucas	
The Black Stallion	**1979**
by Carroll Ballard	
Kagemusha	**1980**
by Akira Kurosawa	
The Escape Artist	**1982**
by Caleb Deschanel	
Hammett	**1982**
by Wim Wenders	
The Black Stallion	
Returns	**1983**
by Robert Dalva	
Mishima: A Life in	
Four Chapters	**1985**
by Paul Schrader	
Lionheart	**1987**
by Franklin J. Schaffner	
Tough Guys	
Don't Dance	**1987**
by Norman Mailer	
Powaqqatsi	**1988**
by Godfrey Reggio	
Wait Until Spring,	
Bandini	**1989**
by Dominique Deruddere	
Wind	**1992**
by Carroll Ballard	
The Junky's	
Christmas	**1993**
by Nick Donkin and Melodie	
McDaniel	
The Secret Garden	**1993**
by Agnieszka Holland	
Don Juan DeMarco	**1994**
by Jeremy Leven	
Frankenstein	**1994**
by Kenneth Branagh	
Haunted	**1995**
by Lewis Gilbert	
My Family	**1995**
by Gregory Nava	
Buddy	**1997**
by Caroline Thompson	
Lanai-Loa	**1998**
by Sherwood Hu	
The Florentine	**1999**
by Nick Stagliano	
Goosed	**1999**
by Aleta Chappelle	
Sleepy Hollow	**1999**
by Tim Burton	
The Third Miracle	**1999**
by Agnieszka Holland	

The Virgin Suicides	**1999**
by Sofia Coppola	
CQ	**2001**
by Roman Coppola	
Jeepers Creepers	**2001**
by Victor Salva	
No Such Thing	**2001**
by Hal Hartley	
Francis Ford Coppola	
Presents: The Legend	
of Suriyothai	**2001**
by Chatrichalerm Yukol	
Pumpkin	**2002**
by Anthony Abrams and	
Adam Larson Broder	
Assassination Tango	**2002**
by Robert Duvall	
Jeepers Creepers II	**2003**
by Victor Salva	
Lost in Translation	**2003**
by Sofia Coppola	
Kinsey	**2004**
by Bill Condon	
The Good Shepherd	**2006**
by Robert De Niro	
Marie Antoinette	**2006**
by Sofia Coppola	
Somewhere	**2010**
by Sofia Coppola	
On the Road	**2011**
by Walter Salles	

Selected Bibliography

Olivier Assayas, Lise Bloch-Morhange, and Serge Toubiana, 'Zoetrope Studios: Entretien avec Francis F. Coppola', *Cahiers du cinéma*, 'Made in USA', nos.334–335, April 1982.

Peter Biskind, *Easy Riders, Raging Bulls*, Simon & Schuster, New York, 1999.

Eleanor Coppola, *Notes: On Apocalypse Now*, Simon & Schuster, New York, 1979; republished by Limelight, New Jersey, 1995.

Francis Ford Coppola, 'Diaries 1989–1993', *Projections*, no.3, Faber and Faber, London, 1994.

Michael Ondaatje, *The Conversations: Walter Murch and the Art of Editing Film*, Knopf, New York, 2002.

Gene D. Phillips, *The Godfather: The Intimate Francis Ford Coppola*, The University Press of Kentucky, Lexington, 2004.

Notes

1. Interviewed by Jean-Pierre Lavoignat, *Studio*, no. 28, April 1991, p.126.

2. From the mid-1950s, Roger Corman directed and produced low-budget B-movies made in a few days, such as *Viking Women* or *Teenage Caveman*. He is famous for his adaptations of Edgar Allan Poe, starring Vincent Price (*The Masque of the Red Death*, 1964) and for his talent for creating openings for newcomers; when he moved to Hollywood, he gave many directors, including Jonathan Demme, Monte Hellman and Martin Scorsese, their first work, and there was even talk of a 'Corman school'.

3. He worked on eleven scripts, including John Huston's *Reflections in a Golden Eye* (1967), Sydney Pollack's *This Property is Condemned* (1966), René Clément's *Is Paris Burning?* (1967) and Franklin J. Schaffner's *Patton* (1970).

4. Peter Biskind, *Easy Riders*, *Raging Bulls*, Bloomsbury, London, 2nd edn, 2009, p.34.

5. Lucas had won a grant from Warner Bros. to observe the filming of *Finian's Rainbow*. Impressed by his short, *Electronic Labyrinth: THX-1138 4EB*, Coppola encouraged him to make a feature film. Lucas then participated in the making of *The Rain People* in the undefined role of 'associate producer'.

6. Other projects put aside included a screenplay he had written, *The Conversation*, and one by George Lucas and John Milius (who made *Conan the Barbarian* in 1982) on the Vietnam War, entitled *Apocalypse Now*.

7. 'I believe in America.' It is with these unforgettable words that *The Godfather* begins. A long zoom out reveals the Don listening to the grievances of one of his 'subjects', like a director considering the casting of an actor. 'I believe in America, but I believe in Sicily even more', the complainant seems to be saying. I believe in the Law, but there's nothing to match a vendetta. The only representative of the law is thoroughly corrupt, a captain of police who has been bought off, played by a cowboy, Sterling Hayden, who starred in Nicholas Ray's *Johnny Guitar* in 1954.

8. Abel Ferrara's films on the Mafia would lay down a strong challenge to the Coppola myth by exposing the unbridled violence of capitalism (in *King of New York*, 1990) and the guilt of a family with 'bad' blood (in *The Funeral*, 1996).

9. Filmed in 1974 by Jack Clayton with Robert Redford, with scant regard for the screenplay.

10. The little-known actor Robert De Niro obtained this part. He had been first employed by Brian De Palma, in *Hi, Mom!* (1970), which brought him to Martin Scorsese's notice for *Mean Streets* (1973), where Coppola saw him.

11. Blondness can never be taken for granted by a family with dark hair, like the Coppolas, and it always seems a crucial choice. Take, for instance, the blond femme fatale, dressed all in yellow, in *You're a Big Boy Now*, the dye that symbolizes Ponyboy's rebirth in *The Outsiders*, and the blondness of the sisters (mythical haloed virgins) in Sofia Coppola's *The Virgin Suicides* (1999).

12. A detail added by Coppola in the audio commentary of the DVD published by Paramount.

13. *The Conversation* does not hide this connection: at the beginning, Harry Caul is disturbed by a mimed sequence from the last scene of *Blow-Up*; later, he tries to pick up a woman in a vast deserted room whose columns recall the scattered trees in the park where Antonioni's photographer witnesses the murder.

14. While editing, Walter Murch, a detective like Harry Caul, found among the out-takes another version of the fatal sentence: 'He'd kill us if he had a chance.' That suggests less the fear of being killed than an encouragement to pre-empt it (the subtext being, if we don't kill him, he'll kill us). Murch put the first version at the beginning of the film, and the second at the end, when Caul realizes that he had 'misheard' the conversation.

15. Serge Daney, 'Apocalypse Now', *Cahiers du cinéma*, no. 304, October 1979.

16. Eleanor Coppola records that even at the post-production stage there was still talk of shooting a final scene, with Willard talking to Kurtz's widow and his son (*Notes: On Apocalypse Now*, Limelight, 1995, p. 277).

17. See Michele Halberstadt, 'Entretien avec Stanley Kubrick', *Première*, no. 127, October 1987, p.70, and *Brian De Palma, entretiens avec Samuel Blumenfeld et Laurent Vachaud*, Calmann-Levy, 2001, p.141. De Palma adds: 'I don't think politics is Francis's strong point. Basically, he's not interested in it.'

18. The major addition is the sequence showing the French plantation (25 minutes long), which turns the voyage up-river into a journey back in time. Before it reaches Kurtz, and the mythic time he inhabits, the boat stops at a property, where, like ghosts, its armed owners appear, figures from the war in Indochina.

19. His utopia was the opposite of that of another director, Jean-Luc Godard, who retreated to his house at Rolle, in Switzerland. Godard himself made the comparison: 'Coppola wants to turn his house into a studio. I want to make my studio my house.' Both of them saw video as a new medium, but while one worked at home in an artisanal fashion, the other invited directors to come to visit him. The two men met in Napa Valley. Coppola distributed Godard's *Sauve qui peut (la vie)*(*Every Man for Himself/Slow Motion*) in North America and involved himself in an abortive project, *The Story*, which Godard wanted to make with Robert De Niro and Diane Keaton.

20. The Steadicam is a stabilized camera developed in the 1970s: operated by a cameraman who is moving about, and first introduced in Stanley Kubrick's *The Shining* (1980), it produces a steady image. Its admirable use in *One from the Heart* is less well known and is further evidence of Coppola's interest in technical developments.

21. *Cahiers du cinéma*, no. 334–335, April 1982, p.44.

22. This effect, absent from the 1983 cut, can be seen in the long version published on DVD in 2005, *The Outsiders: The Complete Novel*. This version of the film, extended by 22 minutes, focuses more on the Greasers as a gang, especially by developing the characters of Ponyboy's two brothers.

23. Ponyboy imitates Paul Newman in Martin Ritt's *Hud* (1963), Dallas stretches his arms backwards in a movement that is the opposite of

James Dean's at the end of Nicholas Ray's *Rebel Without a Cause* (1955), Johnny is a copy of the disturbed boy played by Sal Mineo in that film, the two rival gangs recall Robert Wise's *West Side Story* (1961), and so on.

24. The final title reads: 'This film is dedicated to my elder brother, August Coppola, my first and best teacher.'

25. *West Side Story*, and also John Frankenheimer's *All Fall Down* (1962), the story of a teenager infatuated with his brother (Warren Beatty), a matrix as much for his expressionist use of black and white as for the fetishistic repetition of the character's name ('Berry-Berry', endlessly repeated, like 'Rusty James').

26. Especially on Gus Van Sant, in the Wellesian black and white of *Mala Noche* (1985), Matt Dillon in *Drugstore Cowboy* (1989) and the flying clouds that have become his signature, but also in *My Own Private Idaho* (1992), with its exiled Shakespearean king and an absent mother, for whom the characters search for on a motorcycle.

27. Coppola made this episode in the series *Faerie Tale Theatre* with Harry Dean Stanton and Talia Shire during pre-production of *Peggy Sue Got Married*. The story, adapted from Washington Irving, tells how a man wakes up after sleeping for twenty years and finds that his son has grown up. It's a leap forward in time, the reverse of Peggy Sue's journey into the past, but they have the same result: parents and children meet at the same age. In *The Godfather Part II* cross-fades had been used to interweave the lives of Vito and Michael Corleone.

28. Tucker asked if he could leave school and work with his father,

exactly as Coppola's son had asked him. The film is dedicated 'To Gian-Carlo, who loved cars'.

29. There's a big difference between the films signed 'Francis Ford' and those signed 'Francis'. Following *The Outsiders*, the three commissioned films – *The Cotton Club*, *Peggy Sue Got Married* and *Gardens of Stone* – were signed with a bare 'Francis'. In contrast, the films over which he had full control, *Rumble Fish* and *Tucker*, have the 'Ford'. It's worth noting that *Apocalypse Now* dispenses with the 'Ford': Coppola is distancing himself from a film that is bigger than he is.

30. At the last minute Sofia Coppola replaced Winona Ryder, who had fallen ill. Originally credited as 'Domino', we have seen her grow from film to film; she was born in *The Godfather* (she is the baptized child), plays the younger sisters in *Rumble Fish* and *Peggy Sue*, and dies in The The *Godfather Part III*. It is a life in cinema.

31. To prepare for making his film, Coppola looked at all the adaptations of *Dracula*, but also at Orson Welles's *Citizen Kane* and *Chimes at Midnight* (1941 and 1965) and Sergei Eisenstein's *Ivan the Terrible* (1944 and 1958). He noted in his diary: 'The most important thing is remembering how much I loved going to see horror films with my brother.' ('Diaries 1989–1993', in *Projections*, no.3, 1994, p.17).

32. Brando in *The Godfather* and Pacino in *The Godfather Part III* played characters much older than themselves. The parallel editing in *The Godfather Part II* paradoxically follows a young father and his son when mature played by two actors of about the same age, De Niro (thirty-one) and Pacino (thirty-four).

33. We saw Diane Lane at the age of seventeen, in *The Outsiders* and *Rumble Fish*, and then as a young woman in *The Cotton Club*. She appears here, ten years later, as young as ever.

34. The original title is *John Grisham's The Rainmaker*, like *Bram Stocker's Dracula*. Coppola, who had worked in (almost) every genre, was tempted to make a 'John Grisham film'. Hollywood was then under the spell of the novelist, with Sydney Pollack's *The Firm* in 1993 and Alan J. Pakula's *The Pelican Brief* in 1993.

35. His son Roman paid his homage to the Nouvelle Vague with *CQ* (2001); Sofia enjoyed increasing success with *The Virgin Suicides* (1999), *Lost in Translation* (2003) and *Marie-Antoinette* (2006), for which Coppola proudly represented her at the Cannes Festival.

36. The 'forties' style is very different depending on whether it refers to gangster films (*The Godfather*), to Orson Welles (*Rumble Fish*) or to advertising (*Tucker*).

37. On the one hand, the regulars: Walter Murch (sound), Dean Tavoularis (production design) and Barry Malkin (editing); on the other, for example, Stewart Copeland (music for *Rumble Fish*) or Eiko Ishioka (costumes for *Bram Stoker's Dracula*).

38. Francis Ford Coppola, 'Diaries 1989–1993', *op. cit.*, p.22.

39. Interviewed by Cyril Béghin and Stéphane Delorme, *Cahiers du cinéma*, no.651, December 2009.

Sources

Collection BIFI: pp.14, 24, 29 (bottom), 52, 54, 96 (4th col. centre), 97 (3rd col. bottom).
Collection Cahiers du cinéma: inside front cover, pp.2–3, 4–5, 8, 8–9, 10 (top), 10–1, 11, 13, 15, 16–7, 30, 32, 33, 34–5, 37, 38, 39, 40, 41, 42, 43, 44, 46–7, 50–1, 56–7, 58–9, 60, 62, 63, 64–5, 67, 71, 73, 74 (top), 76–7, 78, 79, 82, 83 (bottom), 84, 86–7, 88, 89, 90–1, 92, 94 (1st col.; 4th col. bottom), 95 (1st col. bottom; 2nd col. bottom; 3rd and 4th col.), 97 (1st col.; 2nd col. bottom; 3rd col. top; 4th col.), 98, 99, 103, inside back cover.
Collection Cahiers du cinéma/ D. Rabourdin: pp.53, 97 (4th col. top).
Collection CAT'S: pp.12, 20–1, 22, 23, 25, 26, 27, 45, 68–9, 70, 72, 74 (bottom), 75, 80, 80–1, 95 (2nd col. top), 96 (4th col. top and bottom).
Collection Cinémathèque Française: pp.10 (bottom), 18–9, 29 (top), 96 (3rd col. bottom), 97 (2nd col. top).
Collection Gilles Traverso: pp.6, 94 (2nd col.), 95 (1st col. top). Screen grabs: pp.36, 49, 54, 55, 83 (top).

Credits

© Columbia Pictures/Zoetrope Studios: pp.4–5, 76–7, 78, 79, 98 (3rd col.).
© Columbia/Sony Pictures: cover.
© Constellation Entertainment/Douglas/ Reuther Prod./Zoetrope Studios/Phillip Caruso: p.92.
© Filmgroup Productions: pp.8, 96 (3rd col. top).
© Hollywood Pictures: p.95 (4th col.).
© Hollywood Pictures/Great Oaks/ Zoetrope Studios: pp.82, 83 (top), 98 (4th col. top).
© Mosfilm: pp.9, 96 (2nd col. bottom).

© Paramount Pictures: pp.18–9, 20–1, 22, 23, 24, 95 (2nd col. bottom), 96 (4th col. bottom), 98 (2nd col. top).
© Paramount Pictures/Phillip Caruso: p.95 (3rd col.).
© Paramount Pictures/Lucasfilm/ Zoetrope Studios: pp.64–5.
© Paramount Pictures/The Coppola Company: pp.25, 26, 27, 29, 74 (bottom), 75, 97 (2nd col. top).
© Paramount Pictures/Zoetrope Studios: pp.30, 68–9, 70, 71, 72, 73, 74 (top), 83 (bottom), 95 (2nd col. top), 97 (1st col.), 98 (2nd col. bottom; 4th col. bottom).
© Seven Arts: pp.10, 96 (3rd col. bottom).
© Seven Arts/Warner Bros Pictures: pp.12, 13, 96 (4th col. top).
© Touchstone: p.67 (bottom).
© Touchstone/Brian Hamill: p.67 (top).
© Traverso: pp.6, 94 (2nd col.), 95 (1st col. top).
© TriStar/Zoetrope Studios: pp.60, 62, 63, 98 (1st col.).
© Universal Pictures/Zoetrope Studios: pp.50–1, 53, 54, 55, 56–7, 97 (4th col. top).
© Warner Bros Pictures: p.94 (1st col.).

© Warner Bros Pictures/Zoetrope Studios: pp.14, 15, 96 (4th col. centre).
© Zoetrope Studios: pp.2–3, 8–9, 16–7, 40, 42, 43, 44, 46–7, 49, 52, 58–9, 84, 86–7, 88, 89, 90–1, 94 (3rd col.), 95 (1st col. top), 96 (2nd col. top), 97 (3rd col.; 4th col. bottom), 99, 103, inside back cover.
© Zoetrope Studios/United Artists: inside front cover, pp.33, 34–5, 36, 37, 38, 39, 40, 80, 80–1, 94 (4th col. bottom), 97 (2nd col. bottom).

All reasonable efforts have been made to trace the copyright holders of the photographs used in this book. We apologize to anyone that we were unable to reach.

Opposite page: Tim Roth and Alexandra Maria Lara in *Youth Without Youth* (2007).
Cover: Francis Ford Coppola on the set of *Bram Stoker's Dracula* (1992).
Inside front cover: *Apocalypse Now* (1979).
Inside back cover: Vincent Gallo and Alden Ehrenreich in *Tetro* (2009).

Cahiers du cinéma Sarl
65, rue Montmartre
75002 Paris

www.cahiersducinema.com

Revised English Edition © 2010 Cahiers du cinéma Sarl
First published in French as *Francis Ford Coppola* © 2007 Cahiers du cinéma Sarl

ISBN 978 2 8664 2569 2

Series conceived by Claudine Paquot
Designed by Werner Jeker/Les Ateliers du Nord
Translated by Imogen Forster
Printed in China